Among the Hoods

Harriet Sergeant is a Research Fellow of the Centre For Policy Studies, an independent, right of centre think tank, and she writes for the *Daily Mail* and the *Sunday Times*. She is the author of three previous books, *Shanghai: A history of the city in the 1920s and 30s*, *The Old Sow in the Back Room: An Englishwoman in Japan* and *Between the Lines*, a book about apartheid in South Africa. She lives in London.

Further praise:

'For three years Sergeant opened herself to a portion of life in the violent margins of London's society, and *Among the Hoods* is the result. At its centre is a loose gang of mainly black men from the south London district of Brixton, varying in age from teens to late thirties, making a living through crime. She came to know them well, and even to nourish an affection for the kind of men who had violently attacked her parents: all, especially an adolescent named Tuggy Tug, are evoked with both skill and pathos as they sabotage their own potential for goodness . . . The book's strength is its descriptive passages, especially where she accompanies the young men to job centres and to clubs run by charities, where indifference, form-filling, distrust and, in the case of one charity, embezzlement of funds, appear to be the norm.' John Lloyd, *Financial Times*

'The surprise is not that Sergeant, a white middle-class lady who has previously turned her formidable talent for research and writing o as the history of Shangh the very

current gang issue, but that she does it in such a personal manner – she befriends them and doesn't give up when it all gets tough. She gets in so deep with these boys she is able to authentically reveal why they and others like them behave as they do. I've spent much time with boys like these, but still found Sergeant's story choking. Sergeant dispels the biggest myth around these "bad boys": they are often up to bad stuff but they are not bad from the outset. Gangs are made, not born, and her account of how gang members long to get out of this life but find it nearly impossible to escape makes for tough reading. Sergeant demonstrates that it is possible to get beyond the fears and limitations of these boys' lives and show them real love and care. Reading this book will confront you with some of the realities these boys face. If you only read one book on gangs, let this be it.'
Shaun Bailey, *Evening Standard*

by the same author

BETWEEN THE LINES: CONVERSATIONS IN SOUTH AFRICA
SHANGHAI: A HISTORY OF SHANGHAI IN THE 1920S AND 1930S
THE OLD SOW IN THE BACK ROOM: AN ENGLISHWOMAN IN JAPAN

HARRIET SERGEANT

AMONG THE HOODS

Exposing the Truth About Britain's Gangs

faber and faber

First published in 2012
by Faber and Faber Ltd
Bloomsbury House
74–77 Great Russell Street
London WC1B 3DA
This paperback edition first published in 2013

Typeset by Faber and Faber Ltd
Printed in England by CPI Group (UK) Ltd, Croydon, CR0 4YY
Croydon CR0 4YY

The right of Harriet Sargeant to be identified as author of this work has
been asserted in accordance with Section 77 of the Copyright, Designs and
Patents Act 1988

A CIP record for this book
is available from the British Library

ISBN 978-0-571-28918-9

FSC
www.fsc.org
MIX
Paper from
responsible sources
FSC® C101712

2 4 6 8 10 9 7 5 3 1

For my son

Prologue

At the height of the riots in the summer of 2011, I got a phone call from Mash, an eighteen-year-old member of a Brixton gang who I had befriended three years before. I was on my way to court for the sentencing of the gang leader, a young man known as Tuggy Tug, who was then nineteen. Two other gang members were already in prison. But Mash, Sunshine and Bulldog, the only white member of the gang, were out on the streets.

Mash was watching a mob storm an electrical shop in Clapham, South London. I could hear screams, the wail of shop alarms and broken glass. I assumed that he had followed the other looters inside.

Instead he was staring around in wonder. 'It's the funniest thing, Harry man,' he confided. 'There's all these people I don't know and it doesn't matter. The only people we worry about is the Feds [police]. Today I can go anywhere in London.'

Gang rivalry usually confines Mash to a few streets around his estate. What the riots represented for him was a sudden explosion of freedom. He was mixing with strangers without the fear of being stabbed or shot. Something we take for granted had left him stunned.

Sunshine, seventeen years old, with a gold tooth and stars shaved about his head, was also calling me. He said that the looters 'were not dressed for it. You can see their faces and they don't care.' He, on the other hand, he reassured me, was in his normal criminal clothes, an oversize jacket with a hood. He gave an exclamation. Two minicabs had drawn up packed with loot-ers. Only in London, I thought, do you go to a riot in a minicab.

I told them to go home. Bulldog, tall and thin, with fast, ner-vous hands, then seized Mash's phone and said, 'But you don't do this every day, Harry. It's wild and exciting. You can do it and you don't get arrested.' Mash took back his mobile to shout out, 'The Feds are scared, Harry man. You look in their eyes and a hundred per cent they are scared. These few days, it's our time.'

Half an hour later I arrived in court for Tuggy Tug's sentenc-ing. Here the authorities were still very much in control. Apart from me, there was no one else from Tuggy Tug's life – not one of his fellow gang members, certainly not his family or any of his victims.

At first I found it hard to take the sentencing seriously. The courtroom boasted pink seats and an air of drama – but not for Tuggy Tug's sentencing. Another trial was taking place. He had been squeezed in during a lunch break. Cardboard boxes of files from the other case were everywhere. As we waited to start, the court clerk, a mannish young woman, cleared a space for the prosecution lawyer. He was chatting and exchanging papers with Tuggy Tug's brief. The court clerk looked up and greeted the probation officer, a small, middle-aged black man in a rumpled suit. 'What have you done to yourself?' she said and straight-ened his collar.

She apologised to me for the delay. It was caused by the guard whose job it was to escort prisoners from their cells. 'She works for a private contractor so she has to have her lunch break,' said the court clerk. 'One of his victims, are we?' she asked. I said I was a friend of the prisoner. She looked surprised and moved away.

Then everything happened very quickly. The clerk of the court took her place, the lawyers straightened up and the pris-

2

oner entered, followed by the judge. Tall, old, wearing a wig and purple silk, he first dealt with the escort, by asking pointedly if she had enjoyed her lunch.

My eyes were on Tuggy Tug. Six months on remand, with regular meals and sessions in the prison gym, had transformed him. Instead of the boy I had known, scared, hungry and on drugs, he was bursting with vitality and health. He saw me and smiled so hard his cheeks squashed up like a child's into his eyes. My heart contracted. Memories flooded back. I recalled when I had last seen him and who had been with us. Tuggy Tug might be going to prison but he was, at least, still alive. In honour of his court appearance, he had braided his hair in a series of small, snakelike twists. I wondered if the judge appreciated his efforts.

The judge cleared a space for himself and glanced through his papers. The court fell silent. Then he looked up, fixed his attention on Tuggy Tug and the atmosphere suddenly changed. 'You are a dangerous young man,' he said. 'You have admitted to over a hundred robberies. You are part of a gang culture. You embarked upon a determined course. You felt it your privilege to prey upon people not able to protect themselves. These are all free choices that you have made. These crimes are premeditated and I have little doubt that you are not a follower but a leader.' Tuggy Tug looked taken aback. He had never heard anything like this before. I wondered how much he understood. An inner-city, state-school education had hardly prepared him for words like 'determined', 'privilege' or 'premeditated'. The judge's contempt, however, needed no translation.

The judge reached for the report from probation. 'It is clear that your mental attitude towards your victims is chilling. You admit you feel for those who commit crimes and serve sentences but not for those who have been robbed.' The judge paused then said, 'This report recommends you should be held in prison indefinitely.'

In shock Tuggy Tug's eyes flew to mine. This we had not expected. I barely noticed what happened next, the discussion on sentencing, the passing back and forth of the volume on guidelines. Tuggy Tug's eyes brimmed. He lifted his arm and dragged it across his face.

After he was led away, I remained in my seat. The lawyers and the probation officer left the courtroom. The clerk came over and offered me a tissue.

Everything the judge had said was true. Tuggy Tug had committed those crimes and more. I was under no illusion. He deserved the four-year sentence the judge had finally decided upon. Tuggy Tug was one of those dangerous young men you read about in the news. A year after that court appearance a probation officer described him to me as 'one of the highest risks we have'. I had experienced at first hand what it was like to be a victim of young men like Tuggy Tug and his gang. My parents had been held up and mugged late one evening outside their home. A youth, the same age as Tuggy Tug, had slashed my mother's hands with a knife, trying to get at her diamond ring. Two others had knocked my father unconscious to the ground. Boys like him prey on the young, the weak and the elderly – like my parents. I should be the last person to defend Tuggy Tug.

What is more, I write for the right-wing press and a right-wing think tank. I believe in prison and punishment. But equally I knew the judge had not told the whole truth. How could he? When you know the whole truth of anything, it is difficult to dispense justice – or leave the courtroom untroubled once justice has been done. And in this case I did know the truth.

On the way home Mash rang wanting to know how much Tuggy Tug had got. 'He'll be out in twenty-two months,' he said with a criminal's ability to calculate England's complicated sentencing system in seconds. I remarked that he seemed unconcerned. 'Goin' to prison, it's a part of life, innit?' he said.

Outside, meanwhile, things had become 'scary'. Buildings were being set alight. Mash had been 'hitting a jewellery shop' but now he was calling it a night. 'These are places my mum goes to.' Bulldog, too, was turning in. The couple of laptops he had 'found' turned out to be broken and then were stolen by other looters while he was inside another shop. 'They just pinch your stuff,' he said in astonishment.

Sunshine was also disillusioned. He had watched helplessly as the pawnshop holding his gold chain burnt down. His father, shot dead when Sunshine was twelve, had given it to him. 'I am proper crying,' he said.

He was not alone. The riots of August 2011 saw unprecedented scenes of destruction and mob rule in England. We witnessed a civil war without a cause. We watched terrifying individuals, hoods up and scarves across their faces, burn, loot and kill. We saw this as not so much a race as a class war. The enemy was 'anyone with a shop or small business – you know, rich people', as one teenager put it. With their ferocity and alien values, the rioters seemed to have come from another planet. But they do not. Like Mash, Sunshine and Bulldog, they come from just down the road.

For many people the riots were their first glimpse of our underclass. They were shocked by what they saw. I was not, due to my unlikely friendship with a gang I had first met outside a chicken takeaway on Knight's Hill, South London, three years before.

One

I was standing in the shade of an awning watching a group of boys on the other side of the road intimidate passers-by. They were shouting and laughing, nudging each other, glaring at shoppers or cadging cigarettes. Aged about fifteen or sixteen, they were dressed almost identically in hoodies and baggy jeans hung low. Their high spirits threatened to erupt into violence at any moment. I assumed they were carrying knives or even a gun. They appeared fearless and capable of anything.

At any other time I would have hurried past, head down, a middle-aged, middle-class white woman desperate not to attract attention. But I was writing a report for a think tank. I wanted to know why so many white working-class and black Caribbean boys like them were failing to make the transition to a successful adult life. Finding a gang in this part of London had been easy. It was nerving myself up to start talking to them that was the problem. So I hesitated, half hidden by the awning.

'Come on!' urged Jerome, my guide and a former robber of security vans who I had recently met. Black, in his mid-thirties and with a large shaved head, he worked in a local community centre and had offered to come with me. 'You need to talk to them little boys,' he said and started across the road. Only then did I step from the safety of the awning and follow.

The boys were astonished when we stopped in front of them.

One pushed the others aside and took charge. He refused to give his real name. None of them used their real names. On the streets he was known as Tuggy Tug and no, he replied to my next question, he did not think he was failing at all. 'In this hood I am the best,' he said. 'I live good in the hood. I can honestly say I enjoy the hood now.'

The others all nodded and stepped back to give him space. Up close I could see he was small for his age and his black tracksuit so big he appeared lost inside it. He had a narrow face, a small aquiline nose, plump cheeks and a full, soft mouth. Despite appearing no more than eleven, he was obviously the leader and proud of his gang. 'Everyone who bumps into us says sorry,' he boasted.

He made no secret of his criminality. He showed me that under his black hoodie he wore a red one – in case he needed a quick change of identity. 'I want no one recognisin' me when I about my business,' he said. He explained, eyeing me, that he was on the lookout for someone to mug. I did not understand how someone who looked so childlike could be so predatory.

The others stood and watched in awe as he addressed me. He never stopped talking and moving, energy crackling off him like electricity. You could barely contain him. I asked why none of them were at school. Tuggy Tug immediately took it upon himself to give me an overview of the situation – half of which I could not understand. Jerome had to translate. Tuggy Tug pointed out that he had no respect for his school, which he had all but stopped attending. 'The teachers don't even try. They only care about the wage at the end of the year,' he said dismissively. He went on, 'You can sit on the desk with your shoes off, your socks hanging out, on the phone, doin' your ting [drug dealing] and the teachers won't give a toss.'

His friends all nodded, eager now to contribute. This was a subject that raised strong feelings. They complained about the lack of discipline. 'There's bare [lots of] people in your class just messin' around,' said one mixed-race boy called Sunshine. He had a gold tooth and a wool cap pulled just above eyes the colour and shape of gooseberries. 'You don't feel like you're learnin' so what's the point of goin' to school?' he mumbled, his eyes refusing to meet mine. 'The teachers wouldn't care,' said a thickset boy called Mash who had a square, good-looking face and was rolling a spliff. 'They just stop and sit down and start reading a magazine.'

'Read a magazine!' I said. 'So what do you do?' Mash revealed a slow, beautiful smile. 'Everyone just go out, running around corridors and do what you feel.' Embarrassed at having said so much, he turned away, pulling his hood close about his face.

Jiggers, even smaller than Tuggy Tug, with scars on his tiny hands, grabbed a drag from Mash's spliff then elbowed him aside. He had a pinched, watchful expression and looked no more than ten. He said he had problems with his English teacher. 'Why did them teachers keep askin' me questions? They knew I couldn't read but they kept on askin'.' Tuggy Tug, Jiggers, Bulldog and Sunshine all admitted to having trouble with 'them little words'. That is why none of them were in school.

Tuggy Tug did not see this as a problem. Education, he said, was a lie put around by the government to entrap him into a lifetime of paying taxes and car fines. His friends stared at him in admiration. 'He tells it as it is,' urged Bulldog from the depths of his hood as he jigged about on his feet and snapped his fingers at unseen enemies. He was tall and skinny and the only white member of the gang.

Tuggy Tug pointed to a Land Rover pulling up on the opposite side of the street. Even someone like that driver, he said, would be doing something on the side. No one could be 'legit' and survive. 'Look at all them bankers and politicians!' he said, enunciating every syllable with relish. He did not see much difference between himself and them. 'Everyone got a scam going,' he assured me.

Here Jerome, despite being in his thirties, agreed. 'Everyone got their ting,' he explained. Even his friends with jobs sold something on the side. 'Otherwise how are you goin' to pay for all them little extras, trainers for the kids, weed, carnival time?' He pointed out that his parents had worked all their lives in social services, 'but they still not paid off the mortgage'.

'If you do it the government way,' went on Tuggy Tug, 'you will wait until you're eighty by the time you can buy a nice, decent tracksuit.' He paused for a moment. 'I probably be dead by then,' he conceded.

'That's how it goes,' said Bulldog with a sigh.

The only person to contradict Tuggy Tug was Smalls, a huge fifteen-year-old, well over six feet with broad shoulders and a black, impassive face. 'The thing is man,' he remarked to the others, in a voice surprisingly soft and high, 'if you do what a hood nigger does, you're only gonna see hood shit. You get me? You can live your hood life but fam pick up a book blud, you never know what's going to happen for you.' (If you do what everyone does in the hood then you are only going to see the bad things that happen in the neighbourhood. You can go on living as you do now but just open a book. You never know how it will change your life.) I turned to him eagerly. Who had taught him the importance of education? Feltham Young Offenders Institute, it turned out, from which he had just emerged. It had given him a different take on things.

In the absence of education and a job, how did they see their future? Tuggy Tug answered for them all. That did not seem a problem. His heroes were rap stars and the older drug dealers in his area. 'I know a man of twenty-one who owns five houses and he never went to school,' he said.

His methods might be criminal but his ambitions were those of millions of other teenage boys. After five years, he planned to go 'legit', buy a house in the suburbs and play golf all day.

He had been getting increasingly fidgety and now announced he wanted cigarettes and that Jerome should come with him to the newsagent across the street. When they got back, Jerome said we ought to leave. As we drove away he explained Tuggy Tug had 'clocked' my watch and suggested in the newsagent's they 'bang' me and steal it. 'Well,' shrugged Jerome, 'he wants a thousand pounds to buy a Smart car. He sees stealing your watch as a career move.'

As he said this, he was rolling a spliff, balancing the Rizlas on his knee. I glanced at it. This was only my second trip to Brixton with Jerome. There were many things I did not understand. Could I be arrested if he smoked a joint in my car and how was I going to get rid of the smell before the school run with my teenage son the next morning?

Instead I asked about the boys' names. 'Well we don't give out our real names. The less you know the better,' said Jerome. His street name was Swagger, 'on account of my flamboyant personality and my designer clothes' – he pointed at his foot and turned it sideways for me to admire. They looked like any other trainers to me. 'Prada,' reprimanded Swagger. He said we should visit the men's department of Prada and Gucci in Bond Street, 'You see all the criminals there.' In his youth he had robbed security vans in order to buy clothes from Prada. I said I had never bought anything from Prada. 'That's the difference between us,' he said. 'With your Princess Di-like background, you can afford to but you don't. I couldn't afford to but I felt bad inside and wearing the clothes made me feel good.'

Why had he felt like that? He lit his spliff, took a deep draw but did not answer. I remarked on Tuggy Tug's energy. 'They will take him in prison and knock it out of him,' said Swagger. 'He'll want to complain. "Certainly," they will say, "fill in this form and we will pass it on," knowing for sure he can't read and write.'

How did he know all this? Swagger offered me his spliff and looked surprised when I shook my head. He took another draw, staring out of the windscreen, then he admitted, 'Cos that's what happened to me when I went inside, innit? That's why I feel bad about myself. I got trouble with all them little words.' At primary school he remembered getting into fights from the age of eight. He was punished by being made to stand in the corridor. 'That didn't help the reading or anything much.' He would forget about the punishment by the next day.

In secondary school, 'I was embarrassed by my reading so I became the class clown.' By the age of thirteen he was bored and frustrated and always in trouble: 'I didn't feel good about myself. I got no pride in myself. I was angry over every single little thing. It didn't take a lot to set me off.' No teacher seemed to notice let alone address the problem. 'So I think why not bunk school and go and do a bit of thieving?'

For a few years it was all 'hustle and bustle', then at nineteen he got caught robbing a security van. 'Other people go from school to university. We go from school to prison. I thought I would be dead by forty.' His parents, first-generation immigrants from Jamaica, both with good jobs, had hoped their only son would become a lawyer or a doctor. He shook his head: 'School shatters your dreams before you get anywhere.'

He had finally learnt to read in prison by writing letters to his parents. Nothing seemed to have changed for Tuggy Tug and his gang. 'Sad, innit?' he said.

As we drove, Swagger drew my attention to places from his youth. 'That is where my friend got shot,' he said of one street corner. A car zipped past. 'That's the flying squad,' he remarked, 'someone's being naughty. Did you see it? No, you don't notice those things, do you?' he added kindly.

I had only stopped for an interview but I could not put Tuggy Tug's hopes for the future out of my head. That middle-class dream of a house in the suburbs and golf at weekends seemed as distant a prospect for Tuggy Tug as becoming an astronaut for the rest of us. I compared him to my fifteen-year-old son.

At that age there were many similarities. Both liked hanging around with their friends in a group on the street – in my son's case even playing rugby there at 2 a.m. They used the same slang and dressed the same: hoodies, jeans slung low, underpants on display. They were both bright, articulate and competitive.

There the similarities ended. Over the next three years I watched their lives sharply diverge. Where my son's opened wide with opportunities, Tuggy Tug's closed down. Like Swagger before him, Tuggy Tug had no future. When I met him on that street corner, his future was already wasted. Ahead lay prison, death or, at best, a lifetime on benefits. Over the next three years I was to learn why. I had written reports, done research, listened to experts at numerous conferences and seminars. I thought I knew all the reasons why boys like Tuggy Tug fail. I was wrong. Nothing in my middle-class life or the think-tank world where I worked prepared me for what I now discovered.

It began after that first meeting. Everything Tuggy Tug and his gang had told me proved to be accurate. When I looked into it, I discovered that a third of all black Caribbean boys and over a third of all white boys from a deprived background read and write poorly. At fourteen their reading age is that of an eleven-year-old. One in five has a reading age of nine years old or younger.

When I questioned teaching staff it was the same story. A science teacher in an inner London school said, 'I am so used to teaching fourteen-year-olds who have a reading age of seven that I don't even think of it as strange any more. It has become the norm rather than the exception.' The headmaster of another secondary school said, 'We don't have the budget or the specialists to teach the majority of the first year of secondary school to read and write properly. We would have to take money from somewhere else and change the timetable.'

Illiteracy is a powerful cause of bad behaviour. The US Department of Justice concluded that failing to learn to read at school 'meets all the requirements for bringing about and maintaining the frustration level that frequently leads to delinquency'. This 'sustained frustration' causes 'aggressive antisocial behaviour'. Illiteracy, as Tuggy Tug was to learn, brings a life sentence on the edges of society. Nearly half of the prison population has a reading ability below an eleven-year-old's. That was the first stark truth I took away from my encounter outside the chicken takeaway. I was soon to discover more.

A few months later I returned with Swagger in search of Tuggy Tug. I had interviewed a white gang about crime and wanted to compare their views. The same group of boys was still standing outside the same dreary takeaway. To my surprise Tuggy Tug greeted me warmly, bounding up from halfway down the street and waving his arms in the air. He had not expected to see me again.

What was it like to be a young criminal? Tuggy Tug said, 'It's peak yeah. Peak.' (As in 'peak time' – so it's a rush and a scramble.) He looked at the others for confirmation. 'Be rude [real],' he urged in order to make sure they told me the truth, 'tell her what you have to do for your dough and that. Tell her how you have to nick it or something fam.' They gathered around to describe their crimes, shrugging up their hoodies and slicing at the air with their hands.

'Oh yeah,' they said, 'we do the stabbin' and the shootin'.'

Despite the hard language, they looked drawn. It was about four in the afternoon. My teenage son always wanted food at that time. I asked if they were hungry. The bravado abruptly vanished. 'We are always hungry,' they said.

No adult appeared to look after them – let alone feed them. 'My mum sometimes give me money for a packet of crisps,' Mash volunteered. Jiggers's mother did not even do that. Smalls was in a hostel. Tuggy Tug and Bulldog were in foster care.

I had planned only to interview them again but the crisp story outraged me. They must be fed, I announced. Their demeanour changed. They moved in closer. 'Will you adopt us?' they asked, only half joking. I felt like Mrs Darling overwhelmed by Lost Boys.

I offered to take three of them out to eat. After much discussion, Tuggy Tug chose Mash and Jiggers. He also chose Nando's in Streatham High Street as a place for a treat.

They walked in, heads down, shoulders stiff as if ready for a fight. Mash and Jiggers ignored the menus, leant back in their seats and stared at the floor. Tuggy Tug was all animation. He took charge, addressed the bemused manager as Boss, questioned him closely on the menu and then, without consulting the others, ordered for all three of them.

Over spicy chicken, the three boys explained what being part of a gang meant to them. In the absence of parents, it offered both protection and emotional support. Tuggy Tug said of his companions, 'I get more from these two than I ever did from my family.'

Young teenagers join gangs, they explained, because they are afraid. There is nobody else to protect them, certainly no responsible adult. 'You don't start off as a killer,' explained Mash, 'but you get bullied on the street. So you go to the gym and you end up a fighter, a violent person. All you want is for them to leave you alone but they push you and push you.' Jiggers agreed: 'Bare little boys do anything to join a gang. If you join a gang with a big name people will look at you different, be scared of you.'

All three emphasised the importance of co-operation. 'We are all linked together. We all bring something to the table. One got a knockout punch. Another good with a knife. We all got our little role.' Tuggy Tug pointed to Jiggers: 'If I ever get into a problem, it's him I look to. I know he won't just gas [boast]. This one, he finish the problem. He go the full one hundred per cent. He shank [stab] the man.' Jiggers carried on eating his chips imperturbably. Tuggy Tug continued: 'Everyone got something. We just a mad team.' Mash leant forward. 'You have to know the people, you have to trust the people, because you do everything together. When you stab, you stab together.'

Street gangs, I realised, were just a distorted mirror image of the house system in my son's school where loyalty and team effort were all-important. My son was lucky. His school had given him what he wanted and turned the teenage boy's natural urge to join a group into an advantage. Tuggy Tug, Mash and Jiggers's school had obviously failed to provide them with anything they needed. So they had done it themselves.

Like any public school, they believed team spirit vital for success. Tuggy Tug explained, 'Most boys our age, they not thinking. They do it by themselves.' Mash interrupted: 'You don't make it in this bad-boy business on your own. You get robbed. You get a beef [a fight or an argument] by yourself, you in trouble.'

The three boys had obviously put a lot of thought into their activities. Apart from team effort, they believed in moderation. Most boys were either too 'half-hearted' or went 'over the top'. They took the middle course. When other boys did make money they 'splashed it around'. Mash said contemptuously, 'They don't invest in nothing. You got to invest for success.' I asked what they invested in. 'Skunk and guns,' replied Mash promptly.

They mainly stole from teenagers slightly older than themselves, they explained – a dangerous occupation for them and us. Revengeful nineteen-year-olds have no inhibitions about using guns in public places during the day. Jiggers had been shot at twice outside the B&Q in Norwood. 'The car pulled up on this big high road,' said Tuggy Tug, 'the sun shining and then pop, pop.' A friend and fellow gang member, also sixteen, had been shot in front of them the week before. Jiggers said, 'You never seen anything like it in your life. Half his head had gone. His face had proper dissolved man.'

How did they judge success? Eagerly they turned out their pockets. Each had at least three mobile phones. 'Everything, boxers, socks, I bought myself,' Tuggy Tug said proudly. They had no parent to give them 'a hundred pounds here and there'. Tuggy Tug was clear. Money equalled status. Money was everything: 'The more money you got, the more ratings you got. If you got no money, you got nothing to sell, then you are nothing. If you got something to sell then you are the man.' Mash defined success as having a phone 'ring like mad because I am busy. I got the deals.'

Mash suddenly let out an exclamation of disgust. He pulled a hair out of his plate of chicken. I could not see anything but the other two caught up Mash's indignation with enthusiasm. All three were now gesticulating and shouting. 'Boss Man, Boss Man,' yelled Tuggy Tug. The manager arrived and apologised, which only set them off again. He then brought a fresh portion. It was like taking out a pack of young wolves who, with the slightest provocation, or just because they felt like it, would leap on the table, bite the staff, knock me flying and run howling out of the door.

They ate everything, including the second portion of chicken. I ordered ice cream, which arrived in small terracotta pots. 'Neat,' said Tuggy Tug, holding his up to admire. He then summoned over the boss man again and, this time with the sweetest smile and coaxing voice, asked if he could take it home. When the manager agreed, he punched the air with his fist and shouted 'Yes' so loudly that I, and the people on the next table, all jumped.

Swagger, who was still with us, went out for a smoke. Left alone with the boys, I half joked about keeping my wallet safe. They leant towards me, their faces softening now they no longer had to keep up appearances in front of an adult male. They would never hurt me, they swore. I was a link – defined by Tuggy Tug as 'anyone who help me move forward in my life', as opposed to a liability, 'someone who holds you back', explained Mash. If anyone mugged me, they would get him, they swore, unless, of course, added Jiggers, he was a fellow gang member. Did I need anything stolen, any kind of drugs or perhaps someone 'mashed up'? Or maybe a Disability Parking Permit? For a moment I was tempted, then I shook my head regretfully. Their fence was a white student living in Richmond. He texted them lists of what he wanted stolen: 'DVDs, laptops, mobile phones, sat navs,' said Jiggers. Tuggy Tug, displaying an entrepreneurial spirit, wondered if maybe I had friends who could give them little jobs to do?

Why waste their energy on crime? I wondered. They shook their heads at me. I did not understand. They had stopped attending or had been excluded from school at thirteen or fourteen and been on the streets ever since. They would remain in a gang because they were qualified for little else other than, as Mash pointed out, 'drug dealing and robbin''.

When you are sixteen and without adult care, money is all-important. Tuggy Tug leant forward. 'It's the worst thing in the world,' he explained, 'to wake up in the morning knowing you have not got a little five pounds to eat breakfast.'

I drove them back to their corner where their friends still

waited outside the chicken takeaway. I gave them each some money. Three large black girls in short skirts and hoop earrings were passing. The boys leapt out of the car with a roar. 'Don't spend it on those girls. Make sure you eat properly!' I called out after them. But they were not listening.

Much later I learnt that Tuggy Tug had charged Mash and Jiggers £5 each for choosing them to join our outing.

Two

A few days later I got a phone call from a woman called Patricia who ran a community centre next to the estate where the boys lived. Tuggy Tug and his friends had been talking about this white woman 'who sits on cake' (has money). She wanted to meet me.

I had finished my report but was still curious. I had interviewed boys all over the country, both black and white, who were leading similar lives to Tuggy Tug. But somehow he had stuck in my mind.

I was under no illusion. The likes of Tuggy Tug and his gang are responsible for the majority of crime in our inner cities. During the riots, they were the young men setting our streets ablaze. Apart from terrorism, nothing frightens people more than youth violence and the inability of our institutions to deal with it.

Richard Taylor knows that danger at first hand. He described the 'catalogue of failures' that led to a gang of teenage boys killing his ten-year-old son, Damilola. These were, he said in 2006, 'failures by the system to keep young people in school and off the streets, failure to prevent them from committing crime and failure by their mentors to give good direction and failure by the authorities to catch them sooner'. As a list of what is going wrong with boys like Tuggy Tug, it cannot be bettered.

Society has always had an ambiguous relationship with its young men – especially young men from a poor background. In times of war, we value their aggression, their sense of immortality, their loyalty to one another. But in peacetime, they are at best a nuisance, at worst a threat. How that threat is channelled has tested societies throughout history. But in contrast to the rites of passage of the past, we now leave boys like Tuggy Tug to scramble up any old how.

The institutions that previously socialised and directed young men – the family, the church and school – have either lost or given up authority. For the last forty years the theories of American pedagogues like John Dewey (1859–1952) have heavily influenced educationalists in charge of our state schools. No teacher should act as 'an external boss or dictator'. They are not in school 'to impose certain ideas or form certain habits in the child'. Beliefs like these have hit boys from a disadvantaged background like Tuggy Tug the hardest. One teacher from an inner-city school complained to me: 'I have really gifted black boys who can't communicate. You see them struggling. It is quite often the reason that they get really upset and frustrated.' Yet he thought it 'patronising' to try to correct them.

If a society wants its youth to share its beliefs then it has to have the confidence to articulate those values with authority. Unfortunately, too many institutions and individuals have lost that confidence.

In the vacuum – as I saw over lunch – boys like Tuggy Tug have created their own values, loyalties and rites of passage – as feral and murderous as anything out of William Golding's novel *Lord of the Flies*. At the end of that book, an adult appears to restore order to the chaos the boys have created. In real life, adults, as the boys had made clear to me, are too often absent or ineffectual. Nor, unlike previous generations, do rebellious youths simply grow out of it. What happens in their teenage years smashes their lives. This comes at great cost to society and the young men themselves. The failure to make the transition to manhood and a successful adult life leaves them for ever trapped in an extended, semi-criminal adolescence. They remain antisocial, out of work and dependent on welfare. Swagger rolling his spliff next to me in the car, unable to hold down a job for long, wondering what was to become of him, was a prime example. As he admitted, 'I may be out of prison but there is no way out for me.'

He was right, but I did not understand let alone accept the inevitability of their lives – or the forces at work on them.

In common with everyone else, I feared young men like Tuggy Tug. I had seen what one gang had done to my parents. I prayed my son would never come up against the boys I had taken out to lunch. At the same time I was shocked that boys the same age as my son did not have enough to eat. I was touched by how one meal and a little interest had opened them up. I was charmed by their humour and surprised by their intelligence and eloquence. I had not expected either from the hoodies on our street corners. They had thought long and hard about the things we take for granted. Family, love and a future were not a given in their lives.

I had never heard a voice like Tuggy Tug's before. Young men like him only get a platform if they are successful or reformed. That never happened to Tuggy Tug. He had opened my eyes to another world. His sheer energy and desire to succeed suspended my moral certitudes. It was like trying to tick off a hyena or plug a geyser.

It made me want to know who are these young men who have seized our streets and set our cities on fire? What does the off-duty hoodie get up to when he is not 'steaming' buses, mugging children on the way home from school, stealing or vandalising cars, peeing in front gardens, selling drugs on the street corner or frightening people late at night? What does he talk about? Who are his friends and where do his loyalties lie? Does he have a family? Who, if anyone, cares about him? What, if anything, is his moral code? What does he think about in bed at night? How did he get to that pitch of desperation and violence – and what keeps him there?

Is he, really, a bad person?

After that first meal Swagger said: 'At the end of two years one of them little boys will be in prison, one in the mental hospital, one in a designer suit and one brown bread [dead].' He was right but in a way neither of us could have foretold. But then Swagger never imagined he would become part of the story either.

After Patricia's invitation, I rang Tuggy Tug eager to help him but unsure of his reaction. He said he would see me at the centre, which was 'in the hood' – the few streets that he considered his own and where he felt safe.

I had imagined a run-down estate. Instead, in the middle of West Norwood, on a mild day in early January, I found myself turning off a typical inner-city high street into what felt like a country lane. Trees met overhead. Then the trees stopped and an expanse of green opened up. In front rose an enormous hall, its doors and windows boarded up. On one side stretched a meadow. The community centre to which Patricia had invited me was a single small room attached to the hall. Patricia, a forceful black woman in a low-cut black dress belted at the waist, came out to greet me. Both she and Raphael, a tall black man with an imposing face, were volunteers. We paused at the entrance. Tuggy Tug and his friends had smashed a glass panel out of the door. 'I banned them for a month,' said Patricia. I wondered why they were to eager to get in. There was not much inside but a sofa and eight computers, all monopolised by young black girls.

Outside, a group of boys, many of whom I recognised from the gathering at the chicken takeaway, were smoking spliffs and talking into mobiles. From the housing estate behind, the flats racked up above the hall like a series of cliff faces, Tuggy Tug, Mash and Jiggers emerged. They lolloped towards the group, a duck of the chin for greeting as they passed – the most acknowledgement you can hope for, I knew from my teenage son, in front of friends.

I approached. Tuggy Tug immediately busied himself laying out a Rizla in the palm of his hand. I ignored him and addressed the others. Why did they come here? Sunshine, who today had removed his wool hat to reveal a geometric pattern freshly shaved into the stubble on his head, gazed at me, his eyes dull with dope. He nodded. 'There is nothing to do there. Only them little computers.'

Surely a community centre or sports facility existed where they could go instead? Teenage boys need a place offering plenty of activities where they can hang around with friends and meet girls. 'There's nothing,' said the boys. Sunshine said, 'We walk around doing nothing all day.' Bulldog added, 'All day we stand around the shops like or come here.'

Tuggy Tug, reassured I would not prove an embarrassment, now took over the conversation and moved it into his usual high gear. He said, 'The government have not got the point. They build this nice youth club at the old bakery but it attracts people from another area, you get me? If this area had a nice one, it would be all right.' Boys from outside their area meant gang fights. Mash added, 'We never go there.' The others nodded. Tuggy Tug said, 'It's a joke man. It's only open once a week. It's got to be open every day, every day.'

Where did they exercise? Teenage boys need a lot of exercise if they are to stay out of trouble. My son played at least one hour of sport every day and rugby matches against other schools at weekends. Sunshine pointed downwards. 'The streets the only place,' he said. Mash leant forward. 'But if people see black

25

youths tryin' to play on the street, we are guaranteed to get into a problem.'

Sunshine said, 'It's madness out there. It's the front line.' Smalls, listening to all of this without expression, took, as before, a more optimistic line: 'Yeah but on the streets you can meet people who change your life.' They were all now looking at me. Mash said, 'You just spoke to us. We are not rude. We are very polite, straight,' and he gave his marvellous smile then quickly flicked away his eyes.

A car now drew up from which emerged a tall, well-built black man in an expensive suit. A small, middle-aged white woman got out the other side. She wore a shapeless skirt, had a pursed mouth and hair in a sensible cut. Without a glance at the boys, they walked into the centre.

The expensive suit introduced himself as Head of Children's Services for the borough. 'We like to come every spring to see how our stakeholders are progressing,' he said. They stood side by side, their attention fixed on the black girls at the computers.

Patricia said, 'Well this is a surprise.' She pointed at the girls. 'You can see for yourselves we are doing very well with our outreach work. We get the young people in but we haven't got the facilities to do more.' The couple did not question Patricia or the girls. They did not even step into the room. They remained in the doorway, the man beaming affably.

Patricia asked where they were going next. They mentioned the old bakery. 'Have you told them you were coming?' asked Patricia. 'Oh yes,' they said as if this were a good thing. Patricia, who had received no such warning, nodded bitterly. 'I bet they are flying around getting ready. I bet they have been doing that all morning.'

Previously I would have sided with the officials in the doorway, admired the girls and ignored the boys outside as part of the inner-city landscape. But Tuggy Tug and his gang had already changed my perspective. I stepped forward. The boys had told me they never went to the council-run community centre. 'Well we know why that is,' said the woman, speaking for the first time. In this area of so few facilities why was the hall boarded up and the meadow not used? The woman eyed me nastily. 'What is your relationship with those boys?' she asked. 'Have you had a CRB check and what are your qualifications for working with youth? We take the well-being and safety of our young people very seriously in this borough.'

The head of children's services was keeping his eyes on the girls. 'Everyone doing well then?' he said. I asked the woman to at least talk to Tuggy Tug and his gang. She grimaced as if I had offered her a lemon to suck. They left without speaking to the boys.

Patricia said to me, 'The staff at the old bakery can't get the kids in. So they will be running around right now trying to round some up. They will be sticking photographs of their own and their friends' children up on the walls to justify all that money they are receiving from the council.' Patricia, I later learnt, had her own reasons for saying this.

As the couple got into the car, Jiggers opened his zip and peed against a tree. I suddenly got angry, hit him in the chest and shouted at him. 'What are people to think of you?' I said. 'Look at that couple in the car, those white people walking their dogs. What is going through their heads? "That's how all black boys behave? There is nothing we can do about them!"' My temper evaporated. The eight or nine boys had gathered close and were eyeing me from beneath their hoods. Patricia and Raphael had retreated inside. I suddenly felt very alone. Then Jiggers shrugged his shoulders, almost, I realised with surprise, pleased at my reaction. 'A man's got to do his ting,' he mumbled and ambled off.

Raphael now came out and unlocked the doors of the hall. It

was huge and still in good condition with the roof intact, a parquet floor and even a stage. Why, in this deprived area, was it not being used? Raphael had dreams of turning it into a community centre with rooms for the boys who had nowhere to live to stay in. I called in the boys and asked them what they wanted from the hall. My mind was running riot with plays, lectures, badminton, basketball, literary classes and chess clubs.

Tuggy Tug pulled me down to earth: 'Maybe a fridge and you can help yourself to a drink.' He explained he lived in a hostel with nowhere to cook, let alone a fridge to keep juice in. Raphael and I smiled. Tuggy Tug said, 'You think that is a joke? That is a major issue in my life. You don't know what it's like coming home thinking that there's gonna be a drink there and you get that close to your door and you just remember that you ain't got no juice.' The very banality of his dream rebuked me.

Raphael had his own complaint. 'Millions are put aside for youth services,' he said. 'I have yet to meet anyone who does the work. White middle-class people are in charge and you have to offer things that look sexy to them – basket weaving, arts and crafts, museum visits.'

We wandered back outside and stared at the meadow, where residents from the estate were walking their dogs. I said we should do some digging and plant a garden for the spring. To my surprise, Tuggy Tug was enthusiastic. 'I done the gardening last summer,' he exclaimed. He even had some gardening tools. We walked round searching for a possible site. The boys were discussing setting up a stall on the high street and selling their produce.

Raphael saw only the political implication. He complained that any good initiative they started, the council took over. 'Everything has to be controlled so they can be seen to be doing their job and look effective. No real work is done on the ground. But when these young men get in trouble on the streets because they have nothing to do, those officials are not going to the funerals. They are not doing the grieving.' He went back inside.

As I left, Tuggy Tug and Mash had turned into a corner of the building to smoke their spliffs. Sunshine was halfway up a tree, leaning against the trunk and chatting into his mobile phone. No one was peeing.

A few days later I found myself in Brixton on a very different occasion. I had met a documentary maker called Tobias who had recently returned from filming poverty in Africa. He asked me to lunch at a new pizza restaurant that had opened in Brixton Market. 'The owners brought the oven from Naples,' he explained, then added with a smile, 'I am sure you have never set foot in Brixton before, have you?' I looked around. All the other diners were white and so were the staff. 'Not this part,' I admitted.

Afterwards I stayed on to do some shopping. Tobias had an appointment with an international charity. 'Just get on the Tube and you'll be quite safe,' he said.

I was wandering around the stalls, hesitating between six different types of mango. High above the array of fruit, the Indian stallholder shouted down advice. 'Don't you be cheatin' my lady friend,' said a voice next to me and there was Swagger. He was wearing a leather jacket and a green hoodie that bunched up like a ruff around his face. With his shaven head, huge eyes that drooped inwards, wide shoulders and dancer's posture, he resembled a nineteenth-century Pierrot. I moved on to the avocados. Swagger picked up one and squeezed. A small, middle-aged black woman in a raincoat shook her head and said, 'If you want it ripe, you have to wrap it in newspaper and put it in the boiler cupboard. Didn't your mummy teach you that? You don't know your own culture.' Delighted to have drawn her out for me, Swagger grinned, called her Mummy and with more chat and laughter between her and the Indian owner we left, with him carrying my bags.

We walked down the narrow passageways between the shops bathed in an aqueous light from the glass ceiling above. It was a Friday and around us hovered elderly black people, the men in suits, the women in coats and hats. We stopped outside a Caribbean restaurant serving crab cakes and oyster fritters. 'This where you should eat,' said Swagger reprovingly before joking with the owner, a tall black woman in a turban who had been in the same class as him at primary school. 'She gives romantic advice too,' he added. We walked out of the market into Brixton Road, where we came up against a large man with a gold tooth who Swagger suddenly swung a punch at. 'Boxer George,' he said, turning it into an introduction. There was more laughter and enquiries into the health of Swagger's father.

Finally, after further greetings and introductions – Swagger appeared related to, or had been to school with or knew through the community work of his father, a large number of people – we settled in a Portuguese café where Swagger's mother used to take him as a child.

Over cappuccinos and Portuguese tarts I asked why, when he had such a strong family and community, had he taken to crime? He said he was humiliated that he could not read. He felt he was letting down his parents and all their hopes. Becoming a robber after that was a small step. 'And I was in a hurry,' he added. His friend up the road was robbing vans and appearing in smart clothes. Swagger was due to start a plasterer's course, 'but I was greedy'.

Our walk to the café had made me realise that Tuggy Tug and his gang did not exist in a vacuum. Where were their families? Did Swagger know them? He had got to know Jiggers because he used to hang around Swagger's block of flats with some other boys. They peed, left rubbish in the stairwell and swore at Swagger when he told them off. Finally Swagger flung a bucket of dirty water at them. 'Then we got on hi and bye terms.' What about the others? He might know something about Mash but more he would not say. 'You wantin' a piece of the ghetto, there,' he warned.

My phone went off with a text from my fifteen-year-old son. I had asked where he was. 'I am cotchin around Islington' was the response. I showed Swagger. What did it mean? Swagger burst out laughing. 'That's Jamaican for hanging around,' he said. 'Ask him what his cotch is like. Is it clean and nice? A lot of men in Brixton prison started by cotchin' around in the wrong places.' 'Just as well I had my own translator,' I remarked to my son later. Why was a fifteen-year-old fortunate enough to attend private school using Jamaican slang? Boys on the street like Tuggy Tug had been turned into icons despite having nothing – certainly not the future prospects enjoyed by their imitators.

We discussed helping the boys. Swagger said, 'They are doin' bad things but they got a sweet side.' It surprised us both. He did not think they were wicked. He had spent six years in prison so he knew what wicked was really like. His life had depended on recognising it. But they would turn bad if something was not done.

The only boy who scared him was the smallest, Jiggers. 'Did you clock how he said what the shotgun had done to their friend's head? He was loving it.'

We now ordered some wine. Our plans for the boys got more elaborate. We talked of restoring the hall into a community centre with a crèche, salsa classes and dinner on offer every night. We wanted to grow vegetables. But most of all we wanted to change the boys' lives. About that we were both determined. We had not the least idea how to succeed. And neither of us, not even Swagger with all his experience, gave a thought to the danger.

Three

A few weeks later I was standing outside Victoria station waiting for Mash and Tuggy Tug. It was a grey day in February. I had just rung them. 'Well where are you?' I asked. 'Five minutes, Harry,' said Mash. In the background I could hear the screams and shouts that characterised all my phone calls to them. It was as if they inhabited a parallel universe on which I could only eavesdrop.

'Phone me back, I got no credit,' urged Mash. I phoned back. Mash's telephone suddenly switched to a blast of grime music. I tried Tuggy Tug. 'We're there, we're there,' he said. This exchange had already lasted for half an hour. But now they emerged from the gloom of the Tube station, glancing back over their shoulders, black hoods pulled over lowered heads, hands dug into pockets, hips moving with the stiff gait of jackals on edge.

'We got to skank the Tube [travel on it without paying], innit,' said Tuggy Tug when I complained of their lateness and the number of phone calls it had taken to meet up. No, they did not have an Oyster card. What was that? they wanted to know. 'Yeah? but we don't pay for them things. Trains and buses are too teeth [extortionate],' said Tuggy Tug when I explained. So they jumped the barriers instead. Tuggy Tug looked around the grubby buildings that surround Victoria station. 'I never seen anything like this,' he said in wonder. 'This is the real thing, innit?' He dug Mash. 'This is high-class London, fam.'

I asked what 'fam' stood for. 'Family' – Tuggy Tug glanced at me in surprise – 'because he's like my family.'

Tuggy Tug had told me he wanted to eat somewhere 'out of the hood'. I suggested Victoria station because it was only one stop from Brixton. I might as well have suggested the moon.

We walked along the street together, I in a grey suit, the boys in overlarge black anoraks, the hoods up and drawn tight around the face, unsure whether to walk next to me or range in front. Suddenly around the corner appeared Shaun Bailey, a big black man, then the head of a charity and soon to become the Conservative candidate for Hammersmith in the 2010 general election. We embraced and I turned to introduce him to the boys. Tuggy Tug had shot up the pavement. Mash stared mesmerised at Shaun. In the restaurant a few minutes later I pointed out that if Shaun could make it, the son of a single mother from a north Kensington estate, so could they. The success did not interest them as much as his 'fly suit' and 'big man shoes'.

Eating together, I had decided, was a way to help them. Nobody had taught them the basics such as shaking hands, speaking clearly and looking a grown-up in the eye. Understanding what they were trying to say often took two or three attempts. Tuggy Tug would switch from his fast street talk to speaking slowly and patiently as if to a child.

And nobody in their lives appeared to feed them. Tuggy Tug was always hungry. He was undersized and hardly appeared to have gone through puberty yet. Nor had they ever received much praise from an adult. I told them they were bright and could be successful. Knowing how to behave was a start.

This caught Tuggy Tug's attention. He suddenly focused. He was eager to learn anything that he saw as helping him on in life. I showed them the menu and how to call the waiter over to order. Tuggy Tug once again ordered for Mash, questioning the waiter closely.

When his steak arrived underdone Tuggy Tug was disgusted.

He jabbed at it with a knife. Mash leant over to take a look. 'You can see blood fam,' he said. 'Boss Man,' shouted Tuggy Tug in consternation, 'I can't eat this. You can see the blood.' 'You don't want it like the lady's?' said the waiter, pointing at my underdone steak. The boys looked at mine. Mash turned to me. 'Don't it give your belly the runs?' he asked with concern.

The waiter took Tuggy Tug's steak away. When it came back, after careful inspection he ate it with enthusiasm. 'This meal here,' he declared, 'is a meal that's filled me up for like two days, bruv. I couldn't eat for two days that's how big this meal is and I ain't eaten a meal like that.' He lived on takeaways that left him hungry, he explained. 'Feel me, bare pizza and chips, eats like you think it's a joke bruv.' Before I had taken them to Nando's, 'I ain't eaten no proper cooked meal yeah in about seven months. Grinding for that long bruv. Eat the same bullshit food again and again bruv, turn over your belly one more time bruv and that's it.'

This seemed a good moment to suggest a way to make money. What about gardening for the elderly? The mother of a friend of mine who lived in the country had complained she could not find anyone to do her digging. I had immediately thought of Tuggy Tug and his gardening tools. We discussed a van and how much it would cost. But then Tuggy Tug worried he would not turn a profit and even I saw the danger of letting them near anyone's home. What we needed was a garden without a house. Tuggy Tug and Mash were now discussing a drug deal that had gone wrong. I could barely understand a word. What about digging up allotments?

Tuggy Tug was enthusiastic. 'My nan's got an allotment,' he said. I was astonished to learn of the existence of a grandmother. In fact she was his foster mother. He turned her and Swagger – who later he described as his uncle – into the relatives who had never cared for him.

Allotments were obviously the answer. They must advertise, I said, make a poster and stick it up around the allotments. 'But what's our business title?' urged Tuggy Tug. 'L Plate Gardeners,' I said because they were learners. They took to this and we imagined a fleet of vans emblazoned with the logo ferrying reformed boys from South London to grateful elderly people in the Home Counties. Tuggy Tug summoned over the waiter and we ordered chocolate ice cream all round to celebrate.

After pudding, Mash leant forward. 'When you are out with your friends,' he asked, 'what do you do? Is it like with us?' Tuggy Tug was kneeling up beside me, his back to the room, picking his teeth in the mirror. 'Well, they do that in the lavatory,' I said. Without a word, Tuggy Tug took himself off.

When he returned, I showed them the gesture for ordering the bill. Tuggy Tug laboriously wrote in the air until a bemused waiter brought the bill. I then showed them how to check it. Tuggy Tug was surprised I did this. He took the bill from me and studied it. 'They charged you an extra tea,' he exclaimed, delighted at his discovery and that he could do something for me. His expression now changed to one of disgust. 'That's thieving!' he said with all the indignation of a thief. Then the entrepreneur in him took over. He looked around the restaurant, counting the tables and calculating. If they added one small thing to every table, every hour, 'That's serious money,' he announced in admiration.

When I said goodbye to them, they thanked me warmly. Tuggy Tug smacked his stomach and smiled so hard his cheeks blew up like a chipmunk's out of a children's cartoon. 'You are down to earth for a posh person,' he announced before retreating into the dark of the Tube.

So began my friendship with Tuggy Tug and his gang. When I started taking the boys out, I assumed I would be the one doing the influencing. I could not have been more wrong. Before I got to know them, I had been complacent. I pay my taxes. In exchange I assumed Tuggy Tug and his like got looked after. Even if not in education or training, you assume sixteen-year-olds can read and write, have a roof over their heads and have enough to eat. That surely is a given in modern Britain.

But here was a boy the same age as my son waking up in the morning hungry. Here was a boy robbing because he did not get enough to eat. How could this Dickensian world of crime and hunger exist in our welfare state?

Over the next three years I got more and more involved with the boys. All the issues that I had read about, single mothers, absent fathers, lack of education and social mobility, the criminal justice system, suddenly took on new meaning as I encountered not just Tuggy Tug and his gang but their relatives and friends. I also saw how the state deals with these young men as I met their teachers, social workers and lawyers. I entered their world and saw state institutions and charities through their eyes. It was a revelation.

I had lived abroad for fifteen years. I had written books on South Africa under apartheid as well as China and Japan. Back in the UK I wrote reports for think tanks on social issues like immigration, the NHS, the police and the care system. So I assumed I had a good idea of what was going on. But now suddenly my own country seemed a foreign land. I wanted to know why young men with ambition and intelligence were having their lives wasted. Above all I wanted happy endings for these boys who made me laugh and had such a gift with words. I became like a proud mother forever talking about them and boring my friends.

'Why,' asked my son once in exasperation, 'is your mobile phone full of photographs of gang members – but not one of me?'

Four

Winter that first year was still lingering when Swagger discovered he knew Sunshine's mother and took me to visit. Like all the boys in Tuggy Tug's gang, Sunshine had a young single mother. Simone had three sons by three different fathers – all well-known criminals in the area. Sunshine had been born when she was sixteen. Simone was an attractive woman in her thirties, with Sunshine's green eyes framed by a multitude of long, glistening braids each clicking with a bead at the end. Swagger admitted he had always fancied her, but 'she only goes with the real big men'. The sitting room of her council flat boasted a thick-pile carpet, a large plasma TV and, on the side table, a goldfish tank and an empty bottle of Moët & Chandon champagne.

Exhausted by school, Sunshine's seven-year-old half-brother slept on the sofa beside her. Simone bounced her latest baby on her lap, her arms slim and tattooed. At the side table Sunshine carefully folded up a pile of ironed clothes. 'He's a neat freak,' said Simone of him affectionately. This was a side of him I had not seen before. Sunshine had recently been convicted of driving without a licence. Simone shrugged. 'Well he can't read so how's he meant to get his theory test?'

A single mother and an absent father is the cause, we are told, of troubled young men such as Sunshine. Those troubled young men are set to multiply. In the last twenty-five years, the number of children in homes with a single parent like Simone has doubled. To accuse these young girls of being feckless is unjust. They are merely responding to the economics of the situation. They are as much victims of bad schools and the perverse influence of benefits as the boys. Whereas boys take to crime, girls get pregnant.

Politicians denounce men for abandoning their families, but they are thirty years out of date. There are no families to abandon in the first place. Half of single mothers are like Simone. They have never lived with a man and have never worked. The government is their provider. Simone had left school with no qualifications. Having three children allowed her to live in a flat and enjoy benefits to just below what she could have earned on the minimum wage. Why the government is financing this situation is unclear. Research by the Joseph Rowntree Foundation discovered that children with only one parent are more likely to have behavioural problems, do less well at school, have sex earlier, suffer depression, turn to drugs and heavy drinking and get involved with drugs and crime. That was certainly true of Tuggy Tug and his crew.

As a fellow of a think tank I knew all the depressing statistics. But Simone was actually the first single mother I had met. Single mothers like Simone, of course, see the situation differently. She was clear who she blamed for Sunshine's predicament: his school and the lack of anything to do in the area.

She described how she had asked the headmistress of his school over and over why her then ten-year-old son could not read. The teacher told her that Sunshine was really doing fine. 'She said I was making too much fuss.' Sunshine's behaviour deteriorated at secondary school. Unable to read, she recalled, 'He did not want his friends to think he was stupid. He got frustrated.' The school warned her that he was throwing chairs around and endangering others. The school made no attempt to solve the problem by taking the situation in hand and teaching him to read. Instead they threatened to kick him out. 'It was a nightmare. Once he tried to run away. He was sobbing and sobbing. I had to chase him up the road. I thought it was something I had done.'

Sunshine looked embarrassed. Swagger said it had been the same for him. 'Your anger builds up. People are saying all these nasty things about you. Then you start getting into fights. Then you end up with the headmaster. How can you explain at fourteen all what's in your head? It's mad.'

Swagger, warmed by Simone's presence, was talking slow and rhythmically, hands cupped and moving as if he were tossing us golden apples. 'All those well-paid jobs, special needs, teachers, social workers, youth offending teams, prison wardens, they all depend on black boys failing. If we don't keep on failing, what would happen to all those high salaries?'

Simone said the primary-school head had finally admitted that Sunshine's teacher was so bad, 'she might as well have sent the children home for a year'.

'See,' hummed Swagger, 'those teachers are getting good money, holidays and all sorts and when they fail our children it's "Well everyone understands where they are from." If those damn teachers were in a better school, they would have to perform, wouldn't they? They would have demanding parents wanting to know, "So why's my child no high-flyer?"'

Simone jigged the baby, flexed the muscles in her slim, tattooed arms, caught Swagger staring, then turned back to me. Sunshine had begun truanting at fourteen, in Year 9. Simone said, 'It's the school's job to keep him in school. But they don't. My job is to get him up in the morning and get him to school. There should be some way of holding him in.' She went on angrily, 'They never told me he wasn't in school. They sent no notice. They took no action. They didn't even tell me to go to the social. Nothing.' She had been shocked by the lack of discipline in the school. 'They don't have a discipline policy. They just call the police.'

Now she did not know what to do with him. Sunshine refused to go to college; 'I can't sit in one place too long,' he explained. Simone went on, 'You talk and talk and talk until you tired of talking. I don't want to be a lawyer.' She turned to him. 'Just do your ting on the side [sell drugs] and have a job.'

She sighed. 'He's so full of potential and got such manners! Year 7 and 8 he took such pride in his uniform. He's always been a neat freak. I thought he might get a job in Selfridges.' Swagger said he had been thinking of doing the same. She turned towards him.

Without a word Sunshine leant between them, took the baby from his mother and began to play with it on his lap. He was gentle and attentive. Simone went on, 'He's not good with pen and paper. He likes to use his hands. If he had not been cooped up he would have been better. They should have got them out more, taken them away on holidays and at weekends. One day's work experience would have helped.'

Sunshine was holding the baby up in front of him and blowing noisy kisses into its stomach.

Simone complained about the lack of activities for teenage boys and the temptations of the streets. 'I do know what it is like. I been on the streets. I know he thinks I am chatting crap but I don't want the police banging on my door asking me to identify a body.' Swagger nodded sympathetically. Simone said, 'There are no clubs for him to join.' In their absence he spent 'too much time' hanging about with his friends. 'It's boring, they're in each other's faces all the time. That where the violence comes from – boredom. One's got better trainers than another and they kick off. Sunshine gets a lot of hassle because he cares for his stuff.'

She blamed the government for not letting parents discipline their children. 'My mother used to beat me. Beating helps. It got me good. Now you can't say nothing to your children without social services threatening to take them away. He will listen to me but then he goes about his business. Other boys say, "Fuck off mum, get out of my room." What does the government do? They just hand out leaflets. They need to come on the estate and see.'

I asked if she thought her sons lacked a father figure. No one in Tuggy Tug's gang lived with their father. 'Once upon a time I would have said it did not matter. Now I think it's important.' She glanced at Swagger. 'You do need a man around. At least now I have learnt how to treat the next two. I am going to get a lot tougher. These two are in for it. I am going to be firm with them. If they start truanting, there will be blood on the pavement.'

The baby was now gurgling and crowing with delight at Sunshine. Simone started to talk about Feltham Young Offenders Institute as if Sunshine's going there was a matter of course.

Over the next few weeks I rang Tuggy Tug and Mash to find out how the poster was progressing. It ran into an unexpected difficulty. Apart from playing PS3 games, the boys did not know how to use a computer – certainly not well enough to design and print off a poster. 'We got to find a girl,' they explained, 'to do dis ting for us.' Mash with his slow smile and handsome face had a girl who was 'proper on me', so that seemed promising. Then Smalls thought maybe one of his cousins could do it after work one day. The girls were all in school, at college or work. I saw the boys a few times but the poster was never ready or left behind. 'But it looks sweet,' Tuggy Tug assured me.

Mash complained he was having problems with his mum. She was always screaming at him and demanding weed. She accused him of looking like his father and wanted him out of the flat. 'It's something to do with her past,' said Mash philosophically. Patricia had told the council he was homeless and got him a room in a hostel. Would I come and look for him there? I found it in a narrow street of small terraced houses rising up a hill. There was lino on the floors, bare white walls and a strong smell of disinfectant and weed. Mash's room was on the top floor. It was very clean and tidy with a small cupboard, a bed by the window and nothing on the walls. I thought of my son's room, the floor piled with clothes and school papers, the unmade bed, posters on the walls. 'I ain't got no money for that,' said Mash.

We ate in a Chinese restaurant on Streatham High Street. An argument broke out with the waiter over the lack of prawns in a dish. Tuggy Tug and Mash went immediately on the attack like dogs expecting a beating unless they got their bite in first. The level of aggression took me aback. I said they were not on the street here. This world required different weapons. They both had charm – why not use that instead? They looked at me, mystified. What was I doing here if I did not enjoy their company? I asked, adding, 'No one's paying me.' At that time it had not occurred to me to write about Tuggy Tug now my report was finished. Only later did I get angry and want people to know what was happening to boys like him. Tuggy Tug nodded, shoving rice into his mouth. As a child in care, every adult in his life had been paid to be with him. Swagger and I were the only exceptions. He turned to the waiter to ask for more orange juice – '. . . yeah, please man,' he added as an afterthought.

Then, when I least expected it, he pulled out a piece of paper and offered it to me proudly. It read 'L Plate Gardeners No Job 2 Hard'. It was decorated with tufts of grass, a spade and a rake and two mobile phone numbers along the bottom. My eyes watered with emotion. I described them in five years' time: successful entrepreneurs with a fleet of vans.

'Yeah but how much do we get paid like today for all this digging?' asked Tuggy Tug. I said I thought about £30 a day. Both boys, I now noticed, were looking unusually slick. A girlfriend had braided Tuggy Tug's hair into cornrows, on top of which he had perched a new baseball hat in a material that glistened like mother of pearl. Mash had replaced his usual anorak with a leather jacket and a new pair of trainers, the laces tied halfway down the tongue in enormous bows. Tuggy Tug leant sideways towards me and flipped open his back pocket. I caught a glimpse of a wad of notes. He sat back up and grinned. 'I can make three hundred pounds in an hour, Harry. Why would I dig all them hours for a light thirty pounds?'

After we dropped them off, Swagger rang the numbers on the poster – something I had not thought to do. The first was unobtainable. The second was answered with a loud 'Yo.' Swagger put on the prissy white voice he used to take me off: 'Is that L Plate Gardeners? I am interested in some gardening.' There was a stunned silence. 'You are taking me for a waste man, innit?' came the reply.

Swagger handed back my mobile phone which he had been using because, as usual, his had run out of credit. How was it possible to persuade the boys of the importance of education when they could make so much money selling drugs? By the time Tuggy Tug realised, it would be too late. He would be in prison, those teenage years wasted and a dead-end life ahead.

Swagger sighed. He knew all too well what lay in store for Tuggy Tug. 'There are things you don't know at fourteen,' he said. 'You need someone to tell you, if you do this at fourteen your life will be happier. Your life will be better. They should have more power to make you. I am really trying now but it's so fucking hard because it is just too late.'

I realised then what our failing education system had done to these boys. A good education is about values; about fostering self-motivation, discipline and aspiration. Boys like Tuggy Tug either get that from school or not at all. They had never experienced the repetition and effort needed for schoolwork. They had never learnt self-discipline or how to concentrate. It had maimed them as surely as if someone had seized an axe and chopped off a limb. It was the biggest gulf between them and my son. They did not know how to turn a burst of enthusiasm into the day-to-day effort required for achievement and success.

The next time I saw Tuggy Tug he had nothing in his back pocket, his hair was wild and all he had eaten that day was a packet of crisps. Like a gambler, he only remembered the wins.

Five

From then on, I was determined to show Tuggy Tug and his gang that there was a world worth having out there. The poverty of their experience shocked me. Their lives were confined to a few streets and even fewer activities. They rarely went to the cinema. They had never been to a theatre, an art gallery or a museum – even the Imperial War Museum, which was only a ten-minute bus ride from Brixton.

A week after our Chinese meal, I announced this was where we were going next. There followed a silence. The others looked to Tuggy Tug. 'Harry man,' he began, 'I am not feeling it. We don't do museums.' He drew the word out like a note, his soft, full mouth pursed up like an affronted sea anemone. 'We are not on all of that stuff.'

I said it was time they did. I promised we would stay no more than half an hour and then go to lunch. Where should we meet? There was another silence. Finally Tuggy Tug explained that certain people were out to get him. It was too dangerous to take a bus to Brixton, for example. This was a new revelation. Tuggy Tug's criminality had gone up a level. Unknown to me, he was now robbing regularly. At any time, on the bus or in the street, he could come up against his victims, their relatives or friends and there would be 'beef'. It did not occur to me that just by being with him, I was putting myself in danger. Instead I agreed to pick them up in West Norwood.

After an inordinate number of phone calls and a half-hour

wait, Tuggy Tug emerged from the estate with Bulldog followed by Mash, who was trailed by a small boy almost submerged in a puffer jacket. This was his four-year-old half-brother Pocket. Instead of taking him to school, his mother had left him at home when she went to work. 'I did not even know he was there,' said Mash, aggrieved. 'I came down the stairs and there he was, watching the telly.'

Pocket had a milky blob of a face and a small, pursed mouth. I put him in the back, gave him my handbag to guard and described to him the job of a rear gunner. He had to watch our tail and be ready to shoot at all times. When not gunning passing buses and cyclists, he proved very informative. I learnt, for example, Mash's real name and that he had a father who wore a heavy gold chain with a diamond between each link. He also drove a Land Rover Sport with 'privacy' glass. Swagger had warned that Mash was 'of the ghetto' and I should not ask about him. I now wondered if this was what he had meant. I glanced at Mash who was staring out of the window. What kind of father was he? I wondered. What influence did a father like that have over his son?

Pocket took aim at a BMW thudding with music then went on talking. He said that when Mash had asked his father to take him to the park to play, his father had replied, 'Go park your arse.' Pocket repeated this piece of paternal indifference with delight. He explained his own father had a different skin colour from himself and was in prison after 'whacking my mum really hard on the butt'. His father had been put away for other things but, even at four, Pocket knew better than to speak of that.

Everybody, except for Pocket and me, got out of the car with great reluctance. The boys slouched into the main hall, hoods well over their faces, heads down with embarrassment. A sudden shout of enthusiasm from Pocket forced them to look up. They stopped in their tracks, their faces breaking open in wonder.

Tanks, submarines, armoured vehicles and field guns surrounded us. Rockets surged skywards. Planes of every vintage circled overhead. Two hours later we were still there. They wanted to see and try everything. I had long since run out of information.

In the basement we walked through the re-creation of a First World War trench. The others were fighting to use the periscope. Mash hovered silently next to me. I pointed out the soldiers in this trench were only a year older than him. 'They had no choice?' he asked, surprised. 'They could not have run away?' I explained they got shot for desertion. 'Like us,' he said. It took another year, and by then it was too late, before I understood what he meant.

On the top floor Bulldog was much taken by the Spitfire. It was the first time I had seen him drawn to anything British. Despite being white, he had adopted the language and culture of his Caribbean gang. 'That's what we had at school innit,' he had once explained, 'Diwali, Martin Luther King, Ramadan.' But of his own country he knew nothing.

I described the Battle of Britain. He had never heard of it. Young men his age received five hours' training, I said, before being sent up to fight. They had saved the country. Bulldog's face lit up with delight. Here was a novel idea. Behaviour that now led to prison then would have won him adulation and a place in history. 'I would have been good at that,' he declared, bouncing about with excitement. He jabbed at an imaginary German, ducked and spun round to finish him with a sideways kick to the kneecap, from his mouth the sound effects of bone crunching on bone. Out of the corner of my eye, I saw the museum guard step forward. 'You would have been good,' I agreed. 'You would have been a hero then.'

Tuggy Tug, as usual, was more down to earth. He looked with disgust at the fragile little Spitfire. 'Those flyers if the wind blow too hard you end up on the floor bruv, trust me.' He then made himself comfortable on a field gun carriage, puffed out his cheeks, glared at the now hovering museum guard then disposed of the Second World War, 'America and Britain they got a beef with the Nazis,' before moving on to why he admired the States. They gave black artists the opportunity. 'That's why we listen to American music.'

The look of wonder and interest inspired by the Spitfire had vanished off Bulldog's face. He now rapped out, 'I want to let out my anger. Yes, squeezing your breasts so hard might let out the cancer.' Mash nodded a beat then ejected, 'In this neighbourhood ugly bitches don't get the time of day.' When I interrupted, they looked amazed. It had not occurred to them that this might be offensive. They always watched their language around me and never discussed sex – at least in a way they thought I might understand. They returned to their favourite black singer. Mash nodded approval: 'He's a real man,' he said. What did he mean by real? 'I heard no one dis him,' he explained. 'Like your father?' I hazarded but his face closed up.

After that Bulldog went off by himself until it was time to leave. I found him staring at a wooden rowing boat in which a group of men had survived shipwreck. Along the edge, a row of notches represented each day at sea. But it was not their story that gripped him. He ran his hands over the curve of the planks, his fingers tracing the joints. It was the only time I ever saw him calm and focused. 'The wood's all right,' he offered. 'I always liked wood.' I asked if he had thought of carpentry. He said he had. He had even been accepted onto a vocational course but at the last minute the company closed it down. They preferred to hire Polish workers who had already done vocational courses back in Poland and did not require the expense of a training scheme.

In the car Pocket thanked me for taking him. He wanted to see everything all over again, right this minute. Mash said, 'Yeah, it was all right,' and Bulldog said he would not mind going again. As Pocket got out, reluctant to leave, dropping the sticks and stones he had collected in the garden afterwards, he formally invited me 'and your children' to his fifth birthday party that Thursday. My heart contracted. He thirsted for knowledge and activity. Had Mash, Tuggy Tug and the others been the same at his age? Would he, in ten years' time, be illiterate and on the street, committing crimes, like his brother? The waste appalled me.

I dropped them at the meadow off Knight's Hill. Swagger was waiting for us. As usual he was beautifully dressed. He might not have money for the Tube or a mobile phone top-up, but his clothes, the result of the occasional modelling job, always shone. Today he was wearing a cream coat with a hood – at least a Bond Street designer's notion of a hood, for this was lined in coyote fur. His head was freshly shaved and gleamed in the cold air. Sunshine was with him, his huge green eyes dope-filled and sad. Swagger said he and Sunshine had something to show me.

They took me to the top floor of a car park and to a small, dirty green car. The back window was torn with bullet holes. A packet of Kleenex lay on the front seat.

'You want to know the hood? This is the stuff that happens Harry man,' said Swagger. 'This what the children that grow up around here have to see, askin' their mums, "What's this, Mum?" And their mums have to lie. Cos this is the front line and these boys are little soldiers around here.'

Swagger rolled a joint and handed it to Sunshine. The two leant against the car, staring out over the wall to a strip of grey sky. Sunshine finally said that his father, who was Swagger's close friend, was shot dead four years before. 'That's why I take this,' he said of the spliff, 'I can't sleep unless I am drowned in it and even then I still don't sleep.' Sunshine's father had been shot in the street. When Sunshine arrived he found blood everywhere. People were walking around covered in blood. They were sitting in their cars and waiting at bus stops covered in blood. The police refused to allow in medical services until they had secured the area. Friends of Sunshine's father kept begging the police to let the ambulance through. They assured the police that the gunman had fled but it still took hours. Sunshine said, 'Is that any way to behave around a dying man?'

Swagger explained that is what often happens when there is a shooting. Now when people call the emergency services after such an event, they always say it's an elderly person or a heart attack. Sunshine recalled, 'As soon as I got there he went as if he had waited for me. That's what I believe anyway.' He had been close to his father. His father took him everywhere. He picked up the then twelve-year-old Sunshine after school, took him to his gym, his boxing club, even on his crime sprees. 'He loved me so much he just wanted me with him. Some of the places,' Sunshine conceded, 'he should not have taken me.' He paused then went on, 'Everything's changed, friends, family, it's not the same since. That big part of the puzzle's gone. It's all been like a muddle.'

Swagger was trying to show me the nature of the world I had now entered. I did not take the danger seriously because my son and his friends were also having their own problems on the streets, being mugged and attacked by other boys. But his troubles were nothing compared to Tuggy Tug's. My son could move freely around London. The lives of Tuggy Tug and his gang were increasingly ringed with fear. 'Man's got to be on his block,' said Tuggy Tug.

On the other side of the road, another gang guarded their block. If Tuggy Tug crossed the road, he risked being stopped and questioned. If he could not say a known name from that block, he was attacked. After one expedition, tired from driving, I asked them to go home on their own. Mash got very upset. Pocket was with him. It meant putting his little brother at risk. It was our biggest falling-out.

It took a long time to understand that we inhabited separate cities. Where I saw Brixton's grand Victorian buildings, its park and rows of terraced houses, they saw a war zone. It was as if I had wandered into one of my son's video games. Familiar streets were suddenly transformed into blasted urban backdrops. Trenches of fire hedged a walk to the bus stop. A traffic island represented a border post, deadly to cross. Popping out for cigarettes involved dodging burning cars and hooded figures who emerged from drifts of smoke, guns blazing. But this was no virtual world. This was their reality.

How had we allowed this to happen? Since when had we abandoned teenage boys to this surreal and terrifying existence? What did it tell them about us – the grown-ups who were supposed to uphold the law and provide protection? 'It weren't like that when I was a youth,' remarked Swagger. 'Back in the day the police tackled gangs.' As well as proper policing, he recalled a five-a-side football tournament made up of youth and police clubs from different areas. 'Obviously that's all stopped,' said Swagger.

Six

It was noticeable that, apart from Sunshine, none of the boys ever mentioned their fathers. In order to get through the dangers of adolescence and into manhood, boys need male role models to emulate and to validate them. One survey of 1,000 parents discovered that one in six children living with a single mother spends less than two hours a week with a male role model, whether a father figure, relative or teacher.

Swagger said it was not always because the fathers did not care. Many of the mothers refused contact. 'Then they get bigger, the mums can't handle them and they call the father. But it's too late. They've not got a relationship.' He was always grumbling about his girlfriend 'going into one', and stopping him from seeing his two-year-old son, Tshane, who he adored. When he turned up on the doorstep with a huge teddy bear for his son, his girlfriend called the police and complained of domestic abuse. Surely she had to have some evidence of injury before he could be charged? He shook his head. She just had to make a claim. 'All them little girls do it,' he said. That was why so many fathers gave up.

Tuggy Tug had started hanging around with a young man called Lips who had a wide smile that cracked open all the sharp angles of his long, thin face. Swagger discovered he knew Lips's father and took me to meet him one cold evening a month after the museum visit.

Jackson was a coke dealer and, apart from Lips, had four children by three different women. He lived in a small block of council flats. Most of these had been bought by their council tenants then sold to landlords who rented them out to immigrants. When we arrived, Jackson came down to let us in, complaining about the group of Polish workers blocking the entrance.

Jackson was small and elegant with the still, angled face of his son. He wore Gucci trainers and a single diamond ear stud. Swagger eyed the ear stud covetously and they discussed who had the best collection of Missoni tops. Shoeboxes containing designer trainers were stacked in the corridor. Jackson admitted there were many pairs he had never worn. But it made him feel good just having them there.

His flat was a combination of opulence and indifference. His bedroom had bare boards, exposed pipes but a coat rail of designer clothes and satin sheets in a leopard-skin print. The sitting room boasted cream leather sofas and a Bang & Olufsen television which remained on throughout the visit. 'I need one like that,' sighed Swagger.

As we talked, Jackson counted out 'sweeties', ecstasy tablets for his night's work, on the coffee table. From where I sat I could see that over the front door, as a precaution against drug rivals, he had slung a machete. His customers were young, white middle-class professionals. He had four phones lined up on the table in front of him. The Bung & Olufsen chirruped continuously.

He explained how he became a father. He would start seeing a woman. Two weeks in and 'bang she gets pregnant'. There is no discussion about it. As far as he is concerned they are barely an item – let alone a family. They are certainly not living together. 'It seems like I am liking her. Then out comes the baby and then we get to know each other a bit more.' He spoke in a bemused way.

But then the relationship 'kicks off', she replaces him with another man and 'then it gets horrible'.

He laid the blame squarely on benefits. 'Women get money

from the government.' More anyway than they could earn from a low-paid job. 'Men get eradicated. What do you need a man for? The government has taken our place. I am old-fashioned, from the ghetto, and I am serious for my kids. But the government is the provider now. What is the result? All these young girls are having babies now. When you have little girls having babies, it's not good, you hearing me? It's not good at all. All these charities, all these government people helping them little girls. But they should be askin': Why are those little girls having babies? What is all the bad things that happen to the kids because them little girls havin' babies without a man? When we were young it was trendy at one stage to have lots of baby mothers. You think it's not going to affect you? Of course it affects you. You see your child suffer and it mashes you up.'

Jackson discovered two of his children were being neglected by their twenty-three-year-old mother. 'Pretty girl,' he said. 'These girls now they taking it to another level. They got the child but the child is a burden. They want to go partying.' She left the children on their own one evening, 'One of my kids turned on a tap and flooded the shop below.' The shopkeeper called the police. They broke down the door, found the children and called social services.

Swagger took out a Rizla, licked then tore off the edge. 'Them young girls got a different style of parenting. They got no standards, no idea,' he announced. Jackson finished sorting ecstasy tablets then produced a small electronic scales and a bag of white powder. A phone chirped and then another. He picked them up and made arrangements for later in the evening.

When the phones fell silent, he sat back, legs sprawled, and nodded at Swagger. 'She fed my kids crappy food and let them fall asleep in front of the TV. There is no routine.'

Social services gave the children to the girl's mother. 'Me and her mum are dealing with the kids. Her mum's good but she feels guilty because she didn't instil no respect and responsibilities into that girl.' When Jackson found out what was going on he rang social services, who then rang the mother. '"Your baby father is very angry," they said. "Is he violent towards you?" he snorted, 'They were trying to make it worse than what it really was. They then investigated me and I felt I was painted with the same brush. I told them, she kept her place like a crack house, dirty clothes everywhere. My boy underweight and quiet.'

Jackson said of his girlfriend, 'I have never seen her look about trying to get back her kids. She's lazy. She's never had a job. She's lived off giros and what men give her.' In order to keep her council flat, she recently had a child by another man. The father of the new baby had a baby from another girl. She told him his new baby mother already had two children in care. He didn't know.

'They were beautiful little kids.' But now he said of his five-year-old son, 'He's angry. It's hard to see a young kid that angry.'

Jackson believed strongly in the power of a good education. He showed me a photograph of his eldest daughter by another woman. She was ten, dressed in school uniform and playing the piano at a school concert. Jackson was paying for her to attend private school. That morning he had taken her to her first day of secondary school. 'The school's wicked,' he said. He thought the expense well worth it: 'They discipline the children. She learns the right values.'

He pointed to the coffee table and explained, 'When she is here, I never discuss business or have weapons or pills lying around. Estate people leave everything in front of their kids, knives, guns, their stash, the lot. Not me.' He nodded emphatically. 'I try and show her the right way. I am there for my kids, definitely there for them.'

A difficult relationship with a baby mother meant he had only got to know his son Lips recently. 'Yeah, he's a good kid,' said Jackson. 'But he needs a spell in prison, you know, to settle him down.'

Seven

Over Easter I had been discussing Tuggy Tug with Tobias, the documentary maker who had taken me to the pizza restaurant in Brixton. His passion to help the dispossessed impressed me. But then he seemed to do all the things that define a good person in our society. He made documentaries on poverty. His friends were human rights activists, heads of charities and even a campaigning pop star. Agreeing with them was tempting. It was like joining a club whose membership guaranteed to the world that you had the right values. I felt in need of guidance. My visits south of the river had begun to confuse me.

During one conversation Tobias said, 'It would be great to give these boys airtime.' He added that I would be key to the project's success. 'Let's hook up at some point soon,' he said.

From this promising start, our phone calls became increasingly strained. Tobias, I soon discovered, might talk movingly of poverty but he did not understand the reality. He also thought he was doing the boys a favour. So he expected them to take the Tube to meet him at places of his choosing and return his calls. But exposing 'how a rigid economic system births all our social problems' was not one of their priorities. 'Man's chatting shit' was how Tuggy Tug put it.

I suggested to Tobias he should stick to his own contacts. There was a silence. It turned out he had none. He talked about institutional racism but, apart from a Nigerian poet, did not know any black people. Finally, after a lot of arguing, he agreed to pay something 'out of expenses' into their bank account. I said they did not have bank accounts. He must pay cash on the day and offer them a meal. He said he would try and remember to bring some sandwiches.

Our conversations had also left him uneasy. My in-depth interview for the film was no longer on the agenda. 'I would say that further down the line, we would certainly need you,' he assured me. We were walking along the canal near Kensal Green Cemetery. Across the water, through the erupting greenery of spring, I glimpsed graves as he talked of poverty and government corruption. On the canal the geese were mating. Suddenly there was a tremendous flap of wings, as one Canadian goose hurled himself at an interloper. I suggested that we invite Swagger to the filming. The thought of spending a day with a former robber of security vans excited Tobias. I was almost forgiven. 'He'll need paying too,' I added.

In the end Tobias preferred to go alone with Swagger to film the boys on their estate in West Norwood. That evening Swagger rang me. He had not taken to Tobias. First Tobias did not bring a car. 'He talked about saving the environment or some such shit,' said Swagger. The roast vegetable, pesto and mozzarella sandwiches had not impressed anyone. Then he had fixed ideas on what he wanted the boys to say. 'He did not want to hear our views,' complained Swagger. It was all about inequality, institutional racism, unlevel playing fields and the *Sunday Times* Rich List. Tuggy Tug's keenness to appear at the top of any such list had not gone down well. After Tobias had finished filming, he made the boys sign a release form. 'What was that all about, Harry?' asked Swagger.

I rang Tobias. A post-performance boredom had replaced his previous enthusiasm. He explained, 'Broadly speaking it says that we are allowed to edit what the boys said in whichever way we choose.' When I questioned this, he talked a lot about film festivals, worldwide screening and a special deal with the States. He promised this would benefit the boys: 'We, unsentimentally, want to help them in whichever way we can.' Had Swagger not appreciated what he was doing for the boys? 'We have offered access to the closed shop that is the film-making world, access to the stand-up comedy world and also to some wonderful coaching networks. Who knows what will come out of that?' He swore he would invite us all to a screening before it was distributed. 'If they see something in there they are not happy with we can sort it out.'

We never heard from Tobias again. We never got to see the film. The boys asked about the coaching a few times then gave up. Tobias was just another grown-up who made promises then disappeared. They had known plenty of those. Sometime later I learnt Tobias had moved to New York and was doing well in marketing.

After that I was much more careful to whom I introduced the boys.

A month later, at the height of spring, I was in West Norwood, this time with a very different documentary maker. Mark was filming a taster for the BBC on gangs. I wanted people to understand what drives boys like Tuggy Tug to crime. That was my intention. It did not quite work out that way.

Things began to go wrong almost immediately. It started with Swagger, who was also to be in the documentary. I had explained to Mark that I would not have got to know the boys without him. Mark and I had arrived at his council block to pick him up. On one side the block enjoyed a sweeping view of London. I had first seen it at night and had stopped, transfixed. I had never looked at the city from that direction before. In the distance the lights of Canary Wharf blinked like jewels. Between stretched an expanse of velvet blackness. Was he not inspired by the view? I had asked Swagger. He had shaken his head. It was the darkness, empty of economic activity, that he noticed. As for the distant lights, 'They might as well be the stars in the sky for all I can reach them,' he had replied.

Now the view was hazy with warmth and the pink smudge of cherry blossom. I went up to get Swagger. The staircase smelt of vomit and pee. I clutched the metal rail, nervous at what lay around the next turn. But as I climbed, a sweet smell from Swagger's bathroom window reached down the last few steps, blotting out the ugliness.

His front door was open and he was standing in his bathroom. It had a cement floor, bottles of expensive bath oils and men's cologne along the windowsill and a half-hearted attempt at tiling up one side. 'My tiler friend never came back to do the corners,' shrugged Swagger. In honour of the filming he was wearing a hyacinth blue-and-white Missoni cardigan over a white T-shirt with jeans and trainers in the same blue. He stepped over the bills and official-looking letters piled on the doormat then closed his front door and locked the iron gate installed after a robbery. Swagger was still indignant at the police's lack of interest. 'I told housing I want to be moved. I don't feel safe no more.'

At the bottom of the staircase someone had delivered a new fridge. Swagger stopped to stare. 'Ra!' he exclaimed. 'I need a fridge.' He got on his phone to call a friend to come over and help him lift it.

I was appalled. 'That's for your neighbour,' I said. 'You can't steal from your neighbour!'

'Why do you think I have that gate?' demanded Swagger. 'They are always stealing from me.' Mark was watching us, bemused. This was hardly the behaviour he had expected from my description of Swagger as a youth worker and research assistant. I wanted to shake Swagger, I was so angry. Swagger now smiled at Mark. 'You going to teach me to roll the camera mate?' he asked. I opened my mouth but then recalled the microphone clipped to my jacket. Swagger returned to fixing a time with his friend when they could carry the fridge to his flat. He glanced at my face. 'Yeah, better make that this afternoon,' he relented.

We got in the car. There was a pause while Mark picked up his camera and Swagger lit a cigarette. Mark asked him to put it out. Swagger assumed he was joking. Mark said he was not joking. I started the engine, but in my agitation stalled then shot onto the pavement, just missing a wheelie bin and an elderly black man. Swagger told me to take more care, still fingering his cigarette, then turned his attention to Mark. 'I need a fridge for when my son comes to stay,' he explained, 'he's only little and they get sick when the milk is off.' Mark said nothing. I stalled the car for a second time.

We now began the laborious business of tracking down Tuggy Tug. 'Is it always like this?' asked Mark. He was not used to people who were being helped making off in the opposite direction. 'Well, he's active isn't he?' said Swagger. 'He don't want to be filmed. I thought they would be on their normal estate in Norwood but our little rugrat has been banned from the area. He is moving from hostel to hostel at the moment. He's shitted on his doorstep so much that he's become known to the police, he's become known to the community and the shop owners they've complained about him. He's had a few arrests and then they put an ASBO on him. They don't want him in the area.'

Happiness animated Swagger's features. He had been nervous of the camera but suddenly he knew this was something he could do well. He raised his hand as he spoke, his fingers moving slowly as if moulding something precious from the air as he explained Tuggy Tug to us.

He went on, 'And then what's dangerous is they've put him all the way up in Thornton Heath. He's not known there so he's got no respect. That's why he didn't want us to go to his hostel. Tomorrow, when he had to go home, he would have been getting scrutinised by other young men, maybe getting into fights or disagreements over "Why was you here with a camera? What was you talking about? Who are you really? Because this isn't your area. You've just popped up in this area, in our hostel and now you're coming with a camera crew."'

When we did finally find Tuggy Tug, he was indeed shocked at the size of the camera, 'the way the camera goes in my face', and Swagger's plan to spend the day by the river in Richmond. 'No please man. I don't want to go to this park blud.' Mark asked if he had seen much countryside. 'Never,' said Tuggy Tug with little sense of loss.

Tuggy Tug too was wearing blue, but unlike Swagger he had dressed for battle. In order to make himself look bigger, he had put on two hoodies, one of wide horizontal blue and white stripes over another of pale grey. In case that did not provide enough cover, he had pulled a blue Nike hat low over his forehead. His mouth was puckering up with disgust and suspicion.

'It's a relaxing vibe,' insisted Swagger.

Tuggy Tug's face lit up with a new idea. 'Let's go to the zoo fam, no river or park, let's go see the giraffes and tigers and that man.'

Swagger and I were laughing. He said, 'This is the first time I've heard you saying that you wanna go to the zoo!'

Tuggy Tug was adamant. This was something he had never done even as a child. He insisted, 'I just wanna go to the zoo and see all the other animals and shit bruv.' Here he made one of his lightning changes of conversation which always delighted me. 'Or can we go to Battersea Dogs Home? I'm down for that bruv a hundred per cent.'

We drove a still-protesting Tuggy Tug to Richmond. I pointed out when he was a successful businessman, Richmond was one of the places he might want to live. Tuggy Tug looked dubious. Swagger said, 'When you start to work you might have something in common with the people around here. Because then you come working-class, innit?' But that prospect held little allure for Tuggy Tug.

'Never. I like the people that I hang around with. I don't wanna be away from them. I feel comfortable with them around me at the moment. And I think I would be comfortable with them in the future cos they're my style innit. My type of thing.'

But then we arrived at the river. At the sight of that lazy loop of water, boats jostling, birds diving, Tuggy Tug fell silent. The belligerence he wore for body armour on the road dropped away. He stared transfixed at a heron. 'That is a big bird you know,' he said.

As on our other expeditions, curiosity took over. He wanted to know about the boats, the length of the Thames, was it a canal and how boats moved along in the water before engines. When I had nothing left to tell him, I bought him an ice cream and he bounded on ahead to watch a scene from a Bollywood movie being shot on the river front.

Swagger and I, now on speaking terms again, were happy to see him relax. Mark was still puzzled. 'I am not sure what he is taking away from it,' he said. My heart sank again. Seeing our friendship with Tuggy Tug through the eyes of an outsider emphasised our lack of expertise or chance of success.

Swagger nodded affectionately after Tuggy Tug. 'I just thought it would be good to take him somewhere different in London. Cos like so many youths in London, they don't get out of their area. They stay trapped in one little zone too, which isn't healthy for them. Cos a little while ago he wanted to go to the zoo and look at the way he's loving it now.'

Tuggy Tug had abandoned the film-makers for a white boy the same age as him who was renting out bikes. Tuggy Tug got down to business. How much did it cost to hire a bike and 'suppose someone borrowed a bike and never paid you back?' The boy explained they required an ID for a deposit. Tuggy Tug went on. How much did he get paid and how old was he? The boy was seventeen and he got paid £50 a day. Tuggy Tug was stunned.

'Fifty pounds a day!'

'Yeah.'

'A day! And that's guaranteed? And you get fifty pounds *today*?'

After that we walked along the river. Mark was still trying to work out the point of the expedition. Tuggy Tug did not give him much help. Did he like being here? 'It's all right,' he conceded. 'It's just here, innit?' But did he find it relaxing? Tuggy Tug thought it might be if he had his friends with him 'and I had money. Then it'd be perfect. But with no money I just don't like to be here. I'm sorry,' he said politely, 'can't be here with no dough.'

Swagger wondered how much money would make him happy. What about £50? Tuggy Tug shook his head, screwed up his eyes and waved his arms. As always he put his whole body into the business of talking. 'No cos fifty pounds is chumpers [small change]. Get a draw, a cab home later and the money would be gone.' No, what he needed was 'Money down fam.' Swagger proposed £10,000 but Tuggy Tug said a 'bag' (£1,000) would be fine. Then he could get his moped. His plans were dictated by the danger he was in on the street. Public transport was just too perilous for him to use.

We sat down on a low wall in the sunshine beneath branches of pink cherry blossom. Tuggy Tug was musing on why he broke the law. 'Yeah, it's not even a crime thing no more, fun doing it fam. It's what man enjoys fam. You feel me? It's gone from like hustle [committing crime because he had to in order to eat]. If I ever get rich yeah I would still do crime. Cos now it's just become like a hobby . . . I enjoy it.' He shook his head sadly. 'Cos I think I enjoy it cos I have nothing else to do.'

Swagger nodded. 'You do it out of boredom.' Tuggy Tug went on, 'I love it fam. I am happy to rob man. I get excited before I rob. I get so happy like yes!'

Swagger asked why he got excited. Tuggy Tug was clear why. 'Girls wanna fuck when man bangs out. If you ain't banging no . . .' he trailed off. Swagger finished, 'Then they don't wanna know you.'

Tuggy Tug's reasons for robbing did not surprise or shock me. They were the same reasons, after all, that drove my son to excel. Teenage boys want to impress girls and win the respect of their peers. My son got that from playing rugby and acting in and directing plays. Many schools understand this need. The then headmaster of Rugby had shown me his job description for new masters. As important as academic qualifications was their ability to run two after-school clubs to a high standard. Without that inspiration and activity, boys like Tuggy Tug organised their own extra-curricular means of attracting girls and admiration.

Swagger sighed. 'If I hadn't stopped robbing security vans, my girlfriend would still be up my arse.'

Tuggy Tug was complaining about the price of bullets. 'Two pound a bullet,' said Swagger, 'is that how much they are?'

Tuggy Tug nodded. 'Two pound a bullet, your life's only worth two pound.' Then he turned to me. 'You don't know how to stroke a poodle?' Even for Tuggy Tug this was a startling change of subject.

I shook my head. A large black poodle bounced past.

'You can't stroke a poodle above the head,' explained Tuggy

Tug. 'You have to stroke underneath.' He gave me an eager smile. 'I'll teach you how to stroke a poodle but you have to ask the lady to control her dog.' I looked to where he was pointing. A lady in a Burberry jacket with grey hair and a no-nonsense air approached us and ordered her dog to sit. She had met Tuggy Tug earlier and had clearly made an impression on him.

Swagger too was respectful. 'He wants to stroke your dog again Miss,' he said. 'Miss' was how he had addressed female prison officers.

Carefully Tuggy Tug patted the dog's flanks, then glanced up at the owner for approbation.

'Yes, if you go like that,' she said.

'Underneath,' said Tuggy Tug to me, 'not over the head.'

I said he was a lovely dog. 'Well trained,' said Tuggy Tug with approval.

On the way up a steep slope in search of lunch, Mark shook his head. 'I am still not sure what he has taken on board,' he said.

A week later Swagger rang me. He had bumped into a deflated Tuggy Tug on the street. He had nowhere to sleep and nothing to eat. Swagger had only £10 in his pocket but nonetheless he bought a takeaway for them both and took Tuggy Tug back to his flat for the night. As I put down the phone, I heard Tuggy Tug complaining, 'I don't even want this dry chicken, blud. I can't eat this dried food,' and Swagger laughing at him. 'Content now? Is your belly content?'

I thought of the many successful men I knew: men of whom the world approved and rightly rewarded; men who moved people with their oratory; knowledgeable men who could fathom future trends and who set up foundations for the poor; men who would never steal a fridge. How many, down to their last £10, would have taken in Tuggy Tug – and done it with love?

And what about Tuggy Tug? Here was a young thug who knew the price of a bullet but whose day was made when a stranger showed him how to stroke a poodle.

I could not make sense of it. I hated crime. I was unprepared to find goodness in criminals. My moral preconceptions were being shot all over the place. I might have failed to influence Tuggy Tug but he was certainly changing me. Nothing I had come across had prepared me for the world I now found myself in.

Eight

By now spring had given way to summer and the weather was warming up. I soon discovered that summer in the inner city is a very different matter. Instead of carefree days and warm nights, it is a time of vigilance and fear. I got an inkling of this when I asked Mash how he planned to spend his summer. Not for him the beach, a summer camp or even a local park. He explained he would be staying put in his room. 'There are too many people out there looking for me.'

In summer boredom drives many adolescents to violence and crime. Jiggers remarked, 'I got stabbed on Friday night. If we had something to do it would not have happened.' Tuggy Tug as usual saw the season as an opportunity. He was determined to get a moped for the summer. 'I'd prefer a bike right now. To be zootin' around.' He explained, 'If you are on a bus in summertime, you can have a hundred guns and you get no respect.' He nodded emphatically. 'I am never going to be hot and bothered on that bus again.' He was to say this every summer but he never actually got his longed-for moped.

Swagger rang me a few days later. He, too, was seeing in summer a chance for improvement. He had been offered a job. The residents of the estate where many of the boys lived had hired Swagger to organise activities for their children. They hoped his 'life experiences', as the association's chairman delicately put it, would see an end to the knifings and car burnings of the previous summer holidays. By life experiences, he meant the six years

Swagger had spent in jail for robbing security vans. Swagger was delighted and saw this as a first step. Fondness for Tuggy Tug and his gang had seen him start a course in youth work. He was full of plans for the future.

The estate was pleasant, with green spaces and low blocks of flats with large windows. The community centre boasted one room barely big enough for its table tennis table and the fifteen or so boys gathered there. Jiggers stood to win £5 if he defeated everyone. He had just seen off Bulldog and had started crowing 'I have won, I have beaten you all' when I arrived. 'Not me,' I said quietly. Everyone looked at me in astonishment. 'Can you play ping pong?' asked Swagger. I started badly and Jiggers relaxed. But then I began to win. Jiggers got rattled. He complained the ball was not the same and changed it. He complained I was making up rules. I realised he was losing face and started to hit the ball out. But he had lost so much confidence; it was hard work to coax a win out of him.

Swagger then announced a game of rounders. We trooped outside. Along the paths between the flats, clothes were drying on railings. Large women, their hair elaborately styled and wearing African costume, stood around and watched us. Enormous numbers of little girls in bright clothes, their hair in elaborate twists and braids, ran in and out of the buildings like flocks of parakeets.

At the back of the estate, between a block of flats and the railway, was a triangle of grass and trees. A Rottweiler, locked on a small balcony three floors up, barked dementedly at us. Swagger staked out the posts and picked two team leaders.

Jiggers was one. He eyed me suspiciously. 'Can you hit a ball? Can you run?' he asked. After the table tennis anything was possible. I shook my head. As the only female, I was the last to be chosen.

My team was mostly younger and smaller than Swagger's and we did not start with much hope. I was waiting to bat behind Jiggers. Despite his age and size, he was the only member of the gang I had not warmed to. Sometimes he even frightened me. He now described how he had been kicked out of his primary school. He had hit his teacher with a bat, 'like this one', which had put her in hospital for two weeks. I said that was outrageous. 'She made me angry,' he replied as if this were reason enough. 'He's got ADHD,' explained the others. 'He can't help himself. He's always whiling out.' Jiggers gave a small, smug smile.

But then he hit a rounder. We yelled as he ran past post after post. He returned transformed and glowing. Bulldog then hit a ball into a clump of daisies and scored another rounder. Now the older boys on Swagger's team lost confidence and began to sulk. Mash climbed up the three floors to the Rottweiler and started to tease him. When I had to leave in order to attend an event at my son's school, they all stopped what they were doing. 'But, like you will be here tomorrow Miss?' they asked. Bulldog walked back with me. 'Rounders is the easiest game,' he said sadly. He yearned for something, apart from crime, to challenge him.

I stopped to chat with Cedric, Swagger's boss and the instigator of the scheme. A large black man in his fifties, he lived in a ground-floor flat. It was the only one with hanging baskets and even a trellis of roses. He complained that none of the mothers did much with their kids, 'and as for the fathers, you never see them'. Two students approached, a Chinese man and a thin, blond German. They were making a film, they explained, and needed a mother pushing a buggy with a child. Cedric pointed to a white boy of about five, sucking his thumb and watching three girls in pink do handstands. The students fell silent. Finally, and with an awful lot of explanation and apologies, they said it had to be a black child.

Swagger's job did not last long. When I rang a few days later, he could barely talk. Jiggers's older brother had accused Swagger of bullying Jiggers. In front of all the children, not to mention Jiggers's mother and her boyfriend, he had attacked Swagger, knocked him down and strangled him until he passed out. Swagger was bitter that his recent training had prevented him from making 'brown bread' of the young man. 'Youth workers don't retaliate. That's what they are telling me. You can never retaliate.' He was not going back. None of the watching grown-ups had intervened.

After this I felt I had to find the boys something to do. I turned to 'Young Lambeth' on the Lambeth Council website and their summer holiday activities programme which promised everything from go-kart tracks to ice-skating. I rang one of the numbers provided; it proved unavailable. I then tried the second. Finally a man with an Indian accent picked up. He was very inquisitive. 'Where are you from? What is your name? Why Lambeth?' I explained I was trying to keep a number of young men out of trouble. He listed everything very fast. I barely understood but managed to catch the mention of a 'sports day'.

'What's the sports day?' I interrupted. That was 'very fun', he assured me, a 'huge event' and free. But after further questions he admitted we had to sign up beforehand and complete mandatory training. I could not see my gang doing mandatory training for anything so I asked about the ice-skating. He said the ice-skating took place in Streatham and I needed to be in a large group in order to attend. In fact, he added, if I wanted to take part in any of the free activities, I needed to be part of a large group.

Instead I found a more hopeful list of things to do from some local charities. Armed with these, I returned to the estate. Swagger met me in the meadow. To celebrate the warm weather, he had put on a yellow T-shirt with 'Elvis' and 'Jesus' in loopy handwriting across the chest, edged in brass beads and sprinkled with pink and gold glitter. He wore yellow trainers to match, a Gucci belt and baggy jeans with large steel zips on the back pockets. He picked at his jeans disconsolately. 'They are last year's,' he said.

After the usual flurry of phone calls, we tracked down the boys to the kitchen in Mash's hostel. It was a soullessly clean and tidy room at the back of a terrace house. A small window looked out over an overgrown garden. About nine teenage boys, including Tuggy Tug, Jiggers, Bulldog, Smalls, Mash and Sunshine, were standing around smoking weed. The air was thick with the smell. It was only 11 a.m. Outside it was a glorious day. The boys said nothing. They just stared at us. For the first time on our adventures, I saw Swagger hesitate, afraid we had walked into a trap. The boys looked on impassive. Fear washed over me. There seemed suddenly so many of them. I froze, afraid if I moved back they would pounce. There was nothing for it but to step forward and smile.

Far from launching an attack, the boys greeted us courteously. What plans had they for the day? I asked. They mumbled and shook their heads. They had nothing planned, they said. They had nothing to do but maybe a little crime later on. I said firmly we would be leaving in an hour.

When we returned the boys had moved to their favourite spot outside some empty garages, the doors ripped off, things rotting in the gloom. Above us rose the flats and overhead walkways of the estate. Swagger explained, 'Those yellow bricks are like heaven to the boys, they feel comfortable once they're in this zone. It's like they really feel at home. They know all the escape routes, the bridges, the alleyways. They know how to get away from the community Feds, where not to be, where not to get caught.'

He recalled his own childhood and using similar bridges and

alleyways on his estate to escape the police. 'They couldn't get hold of us as kids. We'd actually wait for them to come and laugh and taunt them. But in years to come they will hate it around here. They really will. They'll look back and they'll think . . . shit, is this where I grew up? Is this where I loved so much? Look at it. You know?' He gave his sad clown smile then called out to the boys and asked them what they were up to.

They had just stolen a moped from some older boys who had themselves stolen it. To escape identification, despite the sunshine, they were covered up, some in black anoraks, their hoods pulled close around their faces. Tuggy Tug had on his usual dusty blue sweatshirt with a hole in it over which he wore a heavy platinumlike chain. He was leaping about, gesticulating and pointing an imaginary gun at the heads of Mash and Sunshine as they slouched into their hoods against a brick wall.

Mash was wearing a similar chain and I wondered if they had got them in a job lot. He moved a little apart from the others and told me he had turned seventeen the day before. He had received not one birthday card. He added mournfully, 'And I had to go robbin'. Is that any way to spend a birthday?'

A tall, mixed-race young man biked up to speak to Swagger 'about the Princess Diana you are driving around the hood with'. He seemed amiable enough to me but Mash straightened up. 'He's a snitch,' he declared. Tuggy Tug immediately joined him and they glared at the interloper. A few nights before, he and Mash had been hanging around the young man's house. The young man had got so nervous he had called out to his mum, who had promptly gone to the police. Mash sang out with menace, 'He and his mother are both snitches. They goin' to Babylon, goin' down to Babylon.' The young man did not protest. He looked sadly at Swagger and me and cycled off.

Very different was their attitude to Smalls when I offered to take them out for a meal to discuss my list of activities. Unlike the other boys, he wore a dark blue drawstring jacket, zipped up to the chin. It gave him, with his build and muscles gained in the gym at Feltham Young Offenders Institute, an almost military appearance.

Sunshine, Mash and Tuggy Tug were eager to come but were concerned about Smalls. 'Everyone else got his own little ting to do,' explained Tuggy Tug, but Smalls was on his own. I could not imagine that Smalls would have any problems by himself. As usual, I was missing the point. Boys that age are drawn to a small, close group. I explained I could not get all of them into the back of my car. But really I was nervous of Smalls. There followed a lot of anxious discussion. Finally Smalls loomed up above me. 'It's all right,' he said, 'I was not expectin' to come.' His politeness abashed me.

We drove to Clapham. On the way I stopped for petrol. Mash jumped out to help. I told him to fill it up. He looked taken aback. 'But how do I know when it's like full?' he asked then shook his head. 'Not in all my life have I ever seen anyone fill their tank.'

As we drove, the boys looked around fearfully. They were concerned about their safety. 'It makes us boomy, Harry, on the road in summer.' I said they were safe with me. Anyone would have to put a knife through me first. They did not seem convinced by that. I handed them leaflets I had collected on holiday activities in their area – a slot on a radio show, sport, even a competition for young entrepreneurs. Tuggy Tug took one of the leaflets, glanced at where the events took place then shook his head. How could they possibly get to these places? 'Everyone's on the road, Harry. Whatever they are on, they will be on a bit more now. Summer's like motivation,' he explained. 'It's sticky out there. I just stay in my yard, man.' Mash nodded in agreement. 'We just stay in our yard.'

Exactly how much danger were they in? Tuggy Tug, squashed in the back between Mash and Sunshine, said, matter-of-fact, 'Everyone's due a death day but being black and around here, your death day's due soon.'

What was the danger? 'If you're at the wrong place at the wrong time, you lose your life. Say the wrong thing at the wrong time, you lost your life. That quick,' said Tuggy Tug.

Mash said, 'It's a death thing now these days, everyone's just gonna die.'

Had any of their friends died? They ticked off four. One had crashed his moped after being chased by the police. 'Shak got shot in the face and Dre was shot at a disco in Streatham Ice Rink,' said Mash. Another friend: 'He's dead just now,' said Tuggy Tug.

'He died a couple of weeks ago still,' remarked Sunshine.

'He got stabbed in the heart at a party,' said Mash.

'It was mistaken identity,' said Tuggy Tug. 'They thought he was from the next gang. He wasn't even from the gang. So he lost his life.'

They were silent for a moment. Tuggy Tug said, 'Everyone thinking it won't ever be you – just like he did. The day before I see him, I see him there, like right there.' He pointed to the ground. He sighed, 'It ain't hit me, I've got his number in my phone still fam. Like I see him and now he's dead . . . so gone.'

How did that make Tuggy Tug feel? 'It's pissed for him,' said Tuggy Tug.

Did he worry it was going to happen to him?

'Yeah. Every day,' he said. 'Yeah, it's due to happen fam but we don't care about this. We can't be walking around scared every day.'

So how did he keep safe? 'What d'you mean how do you stay safe? Don't slip, you just don't slip. Don't go places where you're not meant to go. Don't walk with the wrong people. Don't go on buses.'

'Don't go to parties,' said Sunshine.

'Don't go to parties at all,' said Tuggy Tug. 'Even if it was on your block.'

But what exactly could happen? Tuggy Tug replied, 'Death you know. It's death that's what everyone fears bruv. You could just die.'

How did they live like that? 'Boy don't know no next way,' he shrugged. 'I live and jam around here so dat's how it has to be like.'

Appalled by this exchange, I took them to a bar with doors wide open onto the pavement and high wooden tables. The walls were hung in a white material and rows of mirrors with ornate silver frames. Lights like stalactites hung from the ceiling in a great burst. We ordered hamburgers and drank watermelon tequilas. Their reactions were typical. Tuggy Tug, ever obsessed with money, called over the waiter to discover the price of the jeroboams on display. Mash had others things on his mind. He looked around. 'You get a girl whipped if you bring her here,' he said approvingly, 'you would get a whole year of loving if you brought her here.'

As we ate, innate good manners saw the boys search for a subject we had in common. They chose crime and skin colour. Racial prejudice, banned from public life, is still alive and well in the criminal justice system. They explained they would never steal from a white, middle-class person like myself because 'We touch you, it's a jail sentence.' Instead they targeted 'a little black man walking with his spliff. We rob him because we know the police won't take it further.'

Tuggy Tug, who had refused to remove his sweatshirt but, as a concession to the heat, had rolled his hat up on one side so it sat turbanlike on his head, now elaborated. He described his idea of a summer activity. The first warm weather had seen them

81

burgle a drug dealer who lived in a hostel. With the same pride and animation with which my son related scoring a try in rugby, Tuggy described the crime. Leaning forward, his cheeks puffed out with excitement, his hands cutting the air, we heard how he had avoided the security cameras, broke into the dealer's room and found £2,500 in cash. On the way in they had been spotted by a passer-by. When they came out, they found the police waiting. 'We were this close, this close, fam,' he said and I caught myself nearly commiserating.

Tuggy Tug described what happened next. 'We were running from the Feds, jumpin' over fences. There were police, dogs, a helicopter . . .'

They were arrested and bailed. Tuggy Tug patted his stomach sadly. 'If we had that money I would have eaten every day in a good restaurant like this. But the Feds got it.' Despite being caught red-handed, 'We got NFA [no further action],' said Mash in stupefaction. The Crown Prosecution Service decided not to proceed with the case. The boys might not have basic table manners, but they knew their legal terms. A week afterwards, 'A policewoman stopped us in the street,' said Tuggy Tug. 'She said the NFA was because we robbed people who were doin' bad tings like ourselves.' So that made it all right.

My attempts to broaden their horizons backfired when we passed a bicycle shop on the way back to the car. Tuggy Tug paused, his attention snagged by the price tag. 'Five bags, fam!' he exclaimed. His friends gathered round and stared at the £5,000 carbon bike. 'That the price of them bare little tings?' asked Tuggy Tug. 'We could just lift one off the road.' Enthusiastically they discussed wire cutters and resale value. They paused to beam at me; the trip, they now all agreed, had been a big success.

They flatly refused to enter the competition for young entrepreneurs.

Nine

Summer in the inner city is not complete without a riot. I should know. I started my own. Until then I had only an inkling of what the boys got up to. Now I found myself not just a witness but taking part in their activities.

I had persuaded Tuggy Tug and Mash to give an interview to the *Today* programme on BBC Radio 4. I was determined that people should appreciate what motivated the boys: the bad schooling, the lack of food or any meaningful activity, the fear. They had been reluctant. The microphone made them nervous and they were anxious not to appear as 'snitches'. Afterwards I offered to buy them each a present. They chose their local JD Sports as the best place to make their choice. So one afternoon in August, I found myself there with Tuggy Tug, Mash, Smalls, Lips and Swagger.

The boys were trying on clothes and shoes, laughing and hollering to each other. I sat down next to Smalls who was sitting silently watching them and played him the clip from the *Today* programme recorded on my mobile. He listened then asked, 'Why are you doin' this?' I said I wanted people to understand them. 'You see, they find you frightening,' I explained, glancing up into his closed, stern face. I added, smiling, 'Aren't you very frightening?' 'I try not to be,' he said.

I urged the others into winter clothes. Tuggy Tug, small enough to browse the junior section, slipped on a child's jacket. It fitted perfectly. He shook his head and pointed to the lining with its tiny green foliage. 'Batty boy [gay] flowers!' he exclaimed in disgust.

Smalls remarked he might not see me for a few weeks. He was going to the country. I was enthusiastic. This was better than smoking dope in the kitchen or stealing bicycles. Was he going on a hike or maybe visiting a farm? Smalls looked at me with incomprehension. He was going to a university town to sell heroin. It was my turn to stare at him. Sixteen-year-old Smalls, whatever his stature, did not fit my preconception of a heroin dealer.

I had begun to think of him as the most mature and thoughtful of the gang. I had even hoped he might study for a degree and had found a charity to help him. Now he was indeed attending university, but not quite as I had imagined. Why did he go? He said because the students, mostly white and middle-class, were good customers. The trip had its dangers. The police had arrested him once already. That was why he had been in Feltham. He sighed: every time he turned up in a small provincial town to sell drugs, the police harassed him. Had he tried dressing differently? He shook his head. How would people know he was a drug dealer if he didn't look the part?

Tuggy Tug and Mash said they did not want a winter jacket. They wanted trainers. I looked down at their perfectly good black trainers – Mash's with large green laces tied halfway down and Tuggy Tug with a flourish of neon blue on his. 'But these are best,' objected Tuggy Tug. 'We want you to buy our second-best.'

As Tuggy Tug walked out with his new pair of second-best shoes, the scanner went off. The manager, a small black man in tinted glasses, went straight up to Tuggy Tug and started shouting in his face. Tuggy Tug leaned into him and shouted right back. The shop assistants, also young black men, started yelling at the other gang members. Outside people stopped and joined in. One shop assistant, a young white girl, hurried up a ladder for safety and called the police.

Feeling responsible, I pushed through and placed myself between Tuggy Tug and the manager. I expected the manager to step back. He did not move. He just leant forward and yelled into my face too. I had never been yelled at like that before. I said if Tuggy Tug had indeed stolen something, I would be the first to call the police. I glanced at Tuggy Tug, who had assumed a martyred expression. 'We are going to strip him,' I announced. Tuggy Tug looked on impassively as I pulled open his jacket and pulled up two hoodies, over which he wore a large silver chain and a T-shirt. Underneath we discovered his trousers half undone. Bunched over them, he was wearing a surprisingly sober pair of underpants in small brown checks. 'Nothing,' I declared.

The manager was still shouting. By now one of the assistants had opened the box of trainers to find the tag still inside. 'See, he's not taken anything,' I shouted. The manager, his face still thrust into mine, yelled back, 'They were in here on Saturday, robbin.' He pulled over Smalls, who loomed above him. The manager was, I had to admit, a brave man.

Unlike the rest of us, Smalls did not lean forward and yell. He stared down from his great height and said softly, 'Are you accusing me?'

I was now seriously worried that Smalls, Tuggy Tug, or, for that matter, I was going to hit the little manager. He would not stop shouting. It was very tiring. I said no doubt Tuggy Tug had been stealing on Saturday but he was not stealing today and the manager should apologise. The manager turned and spat. Smalls went very still. On the pavement scuffles were breaking out. Swagger pointed to the 'Feds' who had arrived and were watching from the other side of the road. Time, I decided, to leave.

Outside Swagger berated the boys. 'They think I am stupid,' he said as we marched along, the new trainers slung over their backs. 'They think I don't know their moves. I made those same moves before they were born. The technology may have changed but not those little moves.' I said of course they had not taken anything. 'One of them is carrying it right now,' exploded Swagger. All four boys stared into the distance.

Tuggy Tug announced he was leaving and turned up a side street. 'He's hungry,' explained Mash matter-of-fact. 'He's goin' to find someone to rob.' Two young men in their twenties walked past. Mash said, 'If you weren't here we would rob them.' I glanced at the men. They were tall and tough with well-developed chests. They towered over my boys. Was that not very dangerous? I asked with concern. Mash shook his head. 'I just look at them and see a large kebab.'

Ten

On my quest to help the boys, Swagger acted as my guide. He became the middleman, explaining us both to each other. It was a role he had played all his life. His parents had provided him with a middle-class upbringing – painting lessons, extra tuition, foreign holidays and museum trips. Then he had gone to prison. His friends included West End actresses, models, church leaders, businessmen and criminals. Reggie Kray had invited him into his cell for tea when they were inmates together at Wayland prison in Norfolk. Swagger was at home everywhere.

It was a role reflected in his choice of language. No one talked as Swagger did. He riffed like a musician through speech patterns, Jamaican Rasta, cockney, South London, upper-class English and just pure Swagger. So on a warm, wet evening in early autumn he announced, 'I am all bubbly, bubbly.'

The occasion was a street party. It was a very Swagger affair. First of all the street party turned out not to be in South London – as I had assumed – but in a designer shop in Bond Street. Through his fashion connections, Swagger had received an invitation to Vogue Fashion's Night Out.

The shop was large and airy with buckets of champagne at the door and the counter tops hidden beneath troughs of orchids. Models sat at small tables scattered around a live band. The lead singer, half Trinidadian and half Swedish, his Rasta locks pulled into a bun at the back of his head, sang so sweetly the models broke off from their texting to listen.

Swagger nodded at a powerfully built black man at the table next to us. He was a boxer who was becoming well known in the area. Swagger told me afterwards, 'Sweets and his crew wanted to take him along on robberies as back-up because he was big. But he was not into anything like that so they brought him to a boxing club and sparred together to toughen him up. That was how he started. Yeah, if he saw Sweets today, he would give him ten grand, that's how much he owes him.'

The place now filled up. Models of every race eddied around us. One, a six-foot blonde with beautiful legs in tiny, jewelled shorts, bent down, flamingolike, in order to talk to three slight men in pork-pie hats and polo shirts. The boxer leant towards Swagger. 'Is your friend still shooting people?' he enquired.

Later Swagger walked me to my car. 'The weather don't look so clever,' he said as it began to rain. He described his most recent attempt at employment. He had joined a charity that put on plays in inner-city state schools. At the first reading, the white playwright sat in the centre with the white director next to him and the black cast, including Swagger, in a circle around them.

The playwright had sought to make his work acceptable to inner-city pupils with language like 'pussy holes'. Everyone nodded approval except Swagger. He said, 'What is this word "pussy holes"? We are putting this play on in schools. There is going to be young girls like my niece who has just started her periods watchin'. What are those young girls goin' to be think-ing?'

The white director said, 'Well, it makes it more real.'

Swagger snorted. 'Murder is real. Rape is real. That does not mean they are acceptable for schoolchildren.'

He shook his head and said, 'It is as if they are locking chil-dren in the ghetto and throwing away the key.' Swagger made an uncomfortable employee. He was too honest and at home in too many different worlds. That job had already ended. 'You will find another one,' I said.

Hanover Square was closed. A man had climbed up a crane and was threatening to throw himself off. 'Silly sausage,' remarked Swagger as he waved goodbye.

After the party, I was all the more determined to show the boys the legitimate life. How could they give up crime when they had no experience of a world without it? I still thought it was just a matter of enlightenment. I did not understand the forces I was up against.

In my innocence I fixed upon the British Museum and the Egyptians. I had been reading the histories of Herodotus, the ancient Greek historian and traveller who clearly describes the Pharaohs as black. Tuggy Tug and the boys had never been to the British Museum and knew nothing of ancient Egypt. I wanted them to see the civilisation these black Pharaohs had created.

I assumed the museum would be interested in us. Government funding for museums is contingent on their outreach work. Tuggy Tug and his gang were about as far out as you can reach. I even daydreamed of our very own guided tour and the boys captivated and enthused.

I rang and asked for advice on how to engage a gang from South London in the museum. Instead of getting an interested response, I was passed from department to department. Somebody offered a schools' pack until they realised I was not a teacher and the boys were not at school. Outreach has its limits, I discovered. I tried the website but it was being refurbished. Finally I ended up talking to a bemused academic in the Department of Ancient Egypt. After a discussion on the Nubian Pharaohs, she, too, passed me on.

Equipped with my copy of Herodotus and photos of the pyramids taken off the Internet, I met Tuggy Tug, Smalls, Mash and Lips at Green Park Tube station. They could just about get to Green Park because it was on the Victoria line. They rejected meeting at a Tube station nearer the museum. They explained it meant a change of line – a manoeuvre they considered beyond them. Swagger had got there earlier in order to enjoy a stroll down Bond Street. He pointed to two men in anoraks sipping coffee. 'They're policemen,' he said. They had clocked him, he explained, and he had let them know he knew they had. 'They been watchin' me till they saw me ring you. Then they knew I had a meeting.' After that they crossed the road to buy a coffee.

I glanced at the men enjoying their drink in the late autumn sunshine. They looked so innocuous. I would never have noticed them before. My trips with Swagger and the boys were increasingly disconcerting. It was as if on impulse I had dived into a submarine world. Things taken for granted on the surface were suddenly reversed. Here it was all icy currents, shadowy predators and walls of coral that plunged into an obliterating nothingness. As I followed Swagger and the boys down, I could not help glancing back, wistful for the surface and the unconcern of the bathers splashing there.

Tuggy Tug had obviously had a good week. He was wearing a new black leather jacket that dipped down at the back. His hair was done in a series of small braids that stuck up, hedgehoglike, all over his head. Over them he had perched at an angle a baseball cap decorated with two large white dice. I said he was looking very smart and he beamed. 'Man's got to keep himself fresh,' he explained. Lips had on a black wool cap pulled low, his usual black anorak, two sizes too big for him, and baggy black jeans. Braids fell on either side of his long, thin face.

The boys were suspicious of my plans and barely bothered to

hide their delight when we found the British Museum closed for security reasons. Swagger suggested a walk around Covent Garden.

We joined the crowds gawping at the living statues, jugglers and tumblers. Swagger paused in front of a young man smoking a cigarette behind a collapsible table. He was a conjurer taking a break. He had a hard, pinched face and gazed indifferently over our heads. Swagger dropped into cockney rhyming slang and cajoled him into starting his routine. The conjurer stubbed out his cigarette and unrolled a black cloth onto the table. His patter had an aggressive edge: 'Have you all gone to sleep? Are any of you watching?' he demanded as he swallowed a pink balloon. Tuggy Tug's mouth slackened in delight. His eyes did not leave the young man's hands. He had, I realised, never watched a conjurer before.

The conjurer called over Tuggy Tug and Smalls and laid out three bronze cups. He asked them to tap on the cup that hid the orange. The boys got it wrong every time. 'Some of us are just very stupid today,' declared the conjuror as oranges now appeared in bewildering numbers from beneath the moving cups then turned into melons and finally a dove.

Afterwards Smalls and Lips approached the conjurer, shoulders hunched with embarrassment, trousers at half-mast, and slipped money into his leather pouch.

We were taking the steps down to a courtyard and a restaurant for lunch when a sound stopped the boys in their tracks. Below us, flouncing about in a jacket and skirt, a woman performed an aria. They gaped at her. They had never heard operatic music before. As we walked past her to lunch, Tuggy Tug held back, scared that her soaring voice would single him out. It was the first time I had seen him at a loss.

Over Sunday lunch the boys discussed religion. I had never

heard my son or his friends discuss God, let alone with the strong emotions of Tuggy Tug and Lips, who both professed to be Muslim. Between them, they had six elder brothers who had all converted to Islam in prison. The boys had scant respect for Christianity. Lips explained to me, 'Them Christians sold people right here in the UK. You seen that programme *Roots*? They sold people as slaves then.' I pointed out Muslims in Arab countries were selling black people as slaves until much more recently. They did not believe me.

Swagger had also converted to Islam in prison. He explained it was because Friday prayers were a good time to see people on other wings and exchange drugs. Nonetheless he pushed the boys on their views. They bandied about Arabic words – none of which I understood. 'What happens when your family is kafir?' demanded Swagger. 'That means when the judgement day comes you will be in heaven and your mother will be in hell.' This struck them all. The mother, however deficient, is sacred. Lips replied in measured tones, 'No one can tell you, not even your mum, if there is a paradise.'

Tuggy Tug, as always, saw the practical benefits. 'If you fast you are forgiven twenty-one sins – even if it's murder. That's what the imam says.'

Swagger shook his head. 'It's not a black man thing,' he said. He pointed out that when anyone enters prison for the first time, 'You are at your lowest and they exploit that.'

The boys jeered at him for not knowing what he was talking about. Stung, Swagger rejoined, 'Don't tell me that. I have worn the T-shirt, taken it off and left it in Wandsworth prison.'

He turned on Lips and attacked the extremism of his mosque. Lips was adamant that no one at his mosque approved of blowing people up. Swagger went on, 'But what happens when you go on a training course and you are in an Arab country and they ask you to do something? Are you going to say no?'

Lips abruptly stood up. Swagger said, 'Are you running from this conversation?' Lips said, 'I am standing up and pulling up my trousers,' which he did and sat down again. Swagger returned to the attack. Why were they not wearing Muslim clothes if they were such believers? 'Why when I ring, don't you say, "Fam ring back, I am prayin' now"?'

Pushed into a corner, Tuggy Tug enunciated his philosophy: 'Stick to your prayers and keep it moving, keep it stepping.'

At the start of lunch, I had unwrapped Tuggy Tug's napkin and handed it to him. He had spread it over his lap, delighted at the concept. Smalls was less impressed. He let his lie over his huge leg then bunched it up and dropped it to the ground.

They left to look around as Swagger and I finished our wine. I said he was too hard on them. His anger surprised me. His affection for the boys was dragging up his own past. He recalled himself at that age and the choices he had made: choices from whose consequences he was still trying to escape. I assumed it was only a matter of time before he got the job and the home his girlfriend wanted. He had begun to suspect otherwise.

Swagger said, 'They're going to remember everything I said to them but when it's too late. That's sad.' He did not understand why they had converted. 'It's bad enough being black in this country without being black and a Muslim. Imagine going to a job interview with that on your CV.' He explained Muslim gangs were responsible for putting drugs and guns into the community. 'If an older man says to these young boys, "There's a non-believer over there who has disrespected my nephew," they will deal with it.' This, he said, was the cause of a lot of black-on-black crime. It had been made clear to him that if he converted, all sorts of opportunities would be open to him. He shook his head. 'They sell heroin right through until fasting time. Soon as Ramadan is over, they start again. What kind of religion is that?

The Muslims laugh at the black guys who turn Muslim. I see it blatant around here.'

A few weeks later I got on a Tube coming back from East London and sat next to an imam. He had a briefcase on his knee and he was reading a religious tract. A young black man in a hood got on at the next stop and sat down opposite us. Swiftly, without anyone in the carriage noticing, the imam got up and passed a pamphlet to the young man. It was about Malcolm X, the black American Nation of Islam minister, civil-rights activist and one-time advocate of violent revolution. Then he took his seat again as if nothing had happened. The young man held the piece of paper awkwardly. Then he slipped it into his pocket and left at the next stop. I glanced sideways. The imam's briefcase was still open on his lap. It was full of pamphlets on Malcolm X. I was about to ask for one too when he noticed my interest and snapped the case closed.

Eleven

Tuggy Tug called me in a state. It was autumn and he was about to turn eighteen. 'Do you know what that means, Harry?' I was nonplussed. For my son, a month older than Tuggy Tug, it meant a big party and being able to get into clubs. For Tuggy Tug, a child in care, it was a very different story.

For the last two years he had lived between hostels and a foster mother. He had once taken me to meet her. She was young and wearing a short, tight skirt. Her flat was spotless and smelt of weed. 'But when I turn eighteen, the council told her they don't give you no more money. She turned me straight out of the house.' He had gone to the local housing office, 'But they can't get me nowhere. So I go all the way over to the next housing and they send me to this other housing. I have to show all these letters,' he said, handling the word as if it might blow up at any moment in his face. 'But I don't even know what they were and that.'

Was he getting any money? I asked. 'I got a little money off my like social worker, a little job-seekers' money and, you know . . .' His normal ebullient voice had turned desperate. 'But it goes on basic stuff like you need that you never had used to buy for yourself. Now you have to.' I asked when he had last eaten properly. 'A good plate of food? Seven days ago.'

Between sixteen and eighteen, young people in care like Tuggy Tug exchange their social workers for a 16 Plus Leaving Care Team, and their foster parent or children's home for independent accommodation. It is, as Tuggy Tug was discovering, a difficult period. There is no going back. Contact with their foster family or former social worker is not encouraged – however well they might have got on. A completely new set of adults looks after them in a new place.

It is a brutal end. We would all sympathise with a sixteen-year-old refugee, separated from family, friends and locality. Yet our government puts young people in its care through similar trauma as a matter of course. Pathway Plans and Special Advisers, as Tuggy Tug was discovering, are small consolation. Where was his Leaving Care Team? Tuggy Tug did not know what I was talking about. 'Maybe in one of them letters?' he hazarded.

I finally tracked down Tuggy Tug's social worker. She was a woman in her twenties. At first she paid lip service to my belief that a successful life depends on forming relationships and that the aim of the care system should be to nourish attachment. It was one of the reasons I persisted in seeing Tuggy Tug. In reality she viewed affection as a nuisance to the bureaucracy. She talked about Tuggy Tug's 'completely fragmented self-esteem' and his 'negative perception' of the care system caused, she admitted, by Tuggy Tug's many changes of foster parents. Yet she saw no irony in the importance of 'trying to break down' any ties Tuggy Tug might have with his foster mother. This was vital if he was to work with 'Our successful Leaving Care Team' and enjoy a bright future of 'cooking skills' and 'learning to keep appointments with social services'. I asked when next she would be seeing Tuggy Tug. There was a pause. Her idea of a relationship was sending him a text every month.

I tried to imagine my son suddenly in Tuggy Tug's position. My son was mature and motivated. But how well would he cope if he had to sever all connection with his family then, in the middle of his A levels, move into a flat on his own and manage on a budget of £44.50 a week?

How well would he handle getting himself up in the morning, eating breakfast and getting to work, school or training on time? Then shopping for his supper on his way home, preparing a meal, doing homework and housework and finally putting himself to bed at a reasonable hour – again on his own? What would happen in an emergency – a stolen wallet, illness, an unexpected bill or ten acquaintances turning up to party? And how would he deal with the loneliness?

I, like many of my friends, did not trust my teenage son alone even for a weekend. Yet here were social workers expecting the most ill-prepared, emotionally damaged and immature teenagers to survive on their own. It is not surprising that two or three years after leaving care the majority are homeless, in prison or, in the case of young girls, pregnant.

For Tuggy Tug it happened a lot sooner. Three days later he and Mash were arrested – Mash for carrying a knife and Tuggy Tug for shooting someone in the face with an airgun in the chicken takeaway. 'We was just foolin' around,' he said indignantly. They were both baffled that two such everyday activities had suddenly landed them in trouble. Neither they nor I had understood the other consequence of turning eighteen. It was finally worth the police's while to prosecute because they would get sent to 'big man' prison.

So began a new phase in our relationship as I saw the institutions that now dealt with young men like Tuggy Tug through their eyes. It proved a revelation.

I told Tuggy Tug off and said I would put together a list of activities and courses for him and Mash. They cancelled at the last minute. I was absurdly naive. I thought it was just a matter of nudging Tuggy Tug into training and a job. Unlike me, Tuggy

Tug had done the maths. He had been to six different schools, had dropped out of education at thirteen, did not know how to use computers, could barely make himself understood to anyone outside his circle and could just about read and write. He knew no one was going to employ him. At the same time he believed it was immoral and the mark of a loser to sign on. Even if he did, how on an income of £44.50, living at that time in a hostel with no kitchen, was he meant to feed himself on three takeaway meals a day? Either he starved or he robbed. It was as simple as that.

He finished our telephone conversation with a hasty 'Nice to speak to you.' He always picked up the phone with a 'Yeah, you all right then?' and used to end with a grunt. Now he had started to copy me.

At least I could do something about Mash. I drove to Balham Youth Court and found him sitting on a bench with his YOT (Youth Offending Team) worker. He was wearing a black leather jacket and new trainers and was slouched low in his seat, his legs spread wide. His YOT worker, an overweight, middle-aged woman, looked me up and down in astonishment. 'You got friends in high places,' she remarked to Mash. She suggested I went in with him. 'They don't see many the likes of you in Balham Youth Court,' she added.

Balham Youth Court is where you get to meet the parents of the young men causing mayhem on our streets. I looked around with interest. Social workers are keen that mixed-race children are adopted or fostered by black couples. The majority of mixed-race boys here were seated next to tired-looking white mothers. An enormous white man with a shaven head in T-shirt and shorts, despite the autumnal weather, discussed his son with their brief. The son was identical to the father right down to the tattoos and piercings. The brief was tall with greying curly hair, worn just too long, and a copy of the *Telegraph* folded beneath his arm. He and the father appeared to be old confederates. Through the open door I saw a white boy lean over the stair rail. He was crying. His father squeezed his shoulder. The boy pulled up the bottom of his T-shirt and angrily wiped his eyes.

As we entered court, I made Mash take off his leather jacket and told him on no account to slouch. Mash and I took our seats opposite three magistrates. It was the first time in court for both of us. We sat bolt upright. I thought if I kept my back straight, it would hold him up too. The magistrates would see the good in him. One lapse of my vigilance, I feared, and back he would slouch into a scowling parody of a hoodie.

The chief magistrate, a thin white man in his fifties, told Mash to stand and confirm his name and address. Mash left out the postcode. The magistrate immediately reprimanded him: 'When I ask for the address, it means the full address,' he said. Mash had been caught carrying a knife. The magistrate announced this to be a serious offence with a custodial sentence. Mash said he was carrying it for defence. I was then asked to address the court. I explained how I knew Mash. The magistrate leant forward. As an author of a think-tank report on black Caribbean and white working-class boys, he said, they would welcome my views. One thing perplexed them – he indicated the two magistrates on either side of him, a woman and an Asian man – why did black boys believe it cool to underachieve?

'Cool!' I said, suddenly very angry indeed. Coolness had nothing to do with it. Was the court unaware of how badly state schools failed these boys? Did they not know the figures on literacy? Were they unaware that it is not difficult to teach children to read and that a lot poorer countries manage better than us because they use traditional methods shunned by many of our schools? Did they not understand how secondary schools, for purely ideological reasons, were failing to give boys like Mash what they needed to thrive – structure, discipline and competitive sports – and that this was the result? The magistrates blinked. They were wondering how to shut me up.

In the end Mash got off. His YOT worker also had given him a good report. They believed he was willing to change, said the chief magistrate. But this was his final chance.

Mash had his own interpretation of the proceedings. 'The judge was feeling you, Harry. I said to myself, "Help yourself, you can feel her a little more if it makes me bust the case."'

Afterwards I drove him to Brixton. He offered to pay for my parking then took me to McDonald's to meet his mother. She had strong features, her hair slicked back, and wore a red coat buttoned tight across her chest like armour. She bought me a cappuccino and a child-sized portion of chicken for herself. She did not offer Mash anything. She worked as a cleaner and did not have much sympathy for Mash. His half-brother Pocket came first. She had thrown Mash out because he was a bad influence on his brother. 'Pocket looks up to you,' she said severely. Mash said he had told the court he was moving back home and would do 'Whatever it takes to keep you happy.'

Briefly her face softened. She said of her oldest son, 'He was so good at primary school, the best at everything.'

Mash said, 'My mum still got a little letter that said how good I was doing. Secondary school, I didn't have many of those.'

She went on, 'It all went to bits in secondary school. I went to speak to the teachers but no one could explain it.'

Mash hunched up his shoulders. 'Nothin' to explain,' he said. 'Every morning I used to meet my friends and goin' down to the caff for a bacon roll. By 10 a.m. everyone coming out of lessons and leaving school and not even a teacher try and stop us. Every morning! You just do what you wanted,' he said in disgust. I was surprised. Had he really wanted the teachers to be strict? Mash nodded. Few people know the benefits of education better than those who have not had one. 'If they had disciplined us, given us a detention, my parents would have come down hard. I would have had to listen.'

Afterwards I insisted we visit Connexions, the government agency that offers advice on education, careers, housing, money, health and even relationships for thirteen- to nineteen-year-olds. I had told the court I would find Mash something to do. I took that promise seriously. His mother showed no interest in coming.

The place was cheerful, with posters, fresh paint and modern furniture. Mash slouched down in a seat and glowered. I looked at this transformation in astonishment. What was the matter? 'I don't like to be kept waiting,' he mumbled. I pointed out he and Tuggy Tug frequently kept me waiting. I did not throw a tantrum, or not often. He grinned and ducked his chin but insisted he did not want to hang around. 'My friends see me here and they will think I am a waste man. Why would you go and humiliate yourself and sign on for fifty pounds a week? That means you are not making no more than fifty pounds. You don't want the street know your humiliation!'

The advisers were all having lunch. We were told to come back in an hour. Finally we were ushered by a large black woman into a cubicle. The woman was solicitous. It did no good. Mash, so good at exercising charm, had transformed into a sullen teenager. She proved more than a match for him. She had been trained to deal with his ilk. She believed this was what he was like.

She extracted from him that he loved football, played for a South London club and had been asked to train as a coach. This last was news to me. How many others had been asked? One other, he replied, resentfully. Out of how many? she pushed. He scowled and slouched lower in his seat. Well maybe more than fifteen, he said, as if she had asked him a tricky calculation. I could have hit him. 'That's very good,' she oozed. Mash stared, mutinous, at the floor.

That over, I now hoped for help. Instead she made another appointment with a different adviser in two weeks' time. 'He is on annual leave now,' she said. In the lobby a young woman was handing out leaflets. She explained she was part of a new initiative, an outreach programme to help young men in gangs 'find a place in society'. She glanced at Mash. 'How did you meet him?' she asked. 'Could you bring in more like him?'

Outside Mash pulled up his hood, shook his shoulders as if shaking off a bad smell and gave me one of his slow, sweet smiles. Afterwards I realised four females had dealt with Mash that morning. The YOT worker, his mother, the Connexions adviser and I had all told him what to do with his life. We had spoken at length and with eloquence. It had got us nowhere. I imagined my son's reaction. A grunt of disapproval from an adult male or Swagger exclaiming 'Bloody Nora' and calling him a 'silly sausage' and Mash would have sat up and listened.

Twelve

A week later I was back in Balham Youth Court for Tuggy Tug's appearance. This was a far less successful expedition. For a start I could not get past the entrance because I did not know Tuggy Tug's real name. 'I have lots of photos of him,' I said, holding up my mobile phone to the security guard on the desk. 'We don't know their faces,' sniffed the man. I rang Mash and woke him up. He laughed, told me Tuggy Tug's real name then urged his friend to 'hold your head up', before falling back to sleep.

I eventually found Tuggy Tug in a side room bursting with energy and talking to his lawyer, a tall young man in a three-piece suit with a bag of files slung over one shoulder.

Tuggy Tug was telling his brief with an air of utter innocence that he was 'doing good' on a Prince's Trust course. I dragged him into a corner. 'You are not on any course,' I said. I explained I would not be speaking on his behalf as I had for Mash. Tuggy Tug had shown no desire to change.

Nonetheless I was anxious. I had grown very fond of Tuggy Tug. Did he think he might go to jail? Tuggy Tug sought to set my mind at rest. 'Me personally I've never been nicked for a big crime. Well,' he amended, 'I've been nicked for a couple of big crimes but I've never been guilty of a big crime. Yeah, touch wood Harry,' and he touched the bench. 'But obviously I've been nicked a lot of times but, like today, always for my puniest shit. You feel me?' I was not sure whether to be reassured by this or not. Tuggy Tug went on, 'So personally I think I am running on luck, Harry man. Love myself to pieces, all that shit yeah,' he added with his most engaging, childlike smile.

Opposite us a black girl in a short green skirt threw a tantrum. She did not want to go into the court. Tuggy Tug was already on the phone to a friend. 'Why is Luella goin' into one?' he said dismissively as she marched out of the building, mother and social worker fluttering around her.

Lips now slouched in and joined us. I said it was nice of him to come. Tuggy Tug explained that his gang, 'They know I don't want to go nowhere on my own. That's why I'm always used to friends cos everywhere I go my friends have been accepted.' He nodded at me approvingly because I had always included them. 'You feel me? That's how me personally, I'm used to having friends around me everywhere I go. I don't go nowhere without no one. I will find someone in their bed at nine o'clock in the morning and swing it around there in a cab and pick them up saying, "Rise and shine. Got court today. Just to follow me."' It was not just friendship. It was too dangerous for him to move around by himself. As he said, 'Not playing games blud.'

Tuggy Tug understood the system a lot better than me. Probation had failed to send a pre-sentence report so he was let off. Just as well, as this time my reception in court was very different. The magistrates, all women, ordered me out. I was neither a social worker nor a relative. I pointed out his social worker had not turned up and he had no relatives. 'But what are you?' they persisted. I left carrying Tuggy Tug's hoodie and jacket with me like the mother of a small child at a children's party.

Afterwards I drove Tuggy Tug back to his estate. Lips had departed unexpectedly to do an errand for his mother. Tuggy Tug and I had not spent much time alone together. We were both awkward. Then I joked about my son and the number of

girls appearing in the house who my daughter and I had chris-
tened the Little Kittens. Tuggy Tug grinned, leant forward and
started to roll a joint. I asked about his family life. 'I never really
had no family like. I grew up on my own you get me. For the
whole of my life that is the God's honest truth.' Like my son, he
found it easier to talk in a car, where he did not have to look a
grown-up in the face.

He laid out the Rizlas on his knee, sprinkled on the tobacco
then retrieved a small ball of weed from inside his trainer. The
drug had been on him, I realised, throughout his court appearance. He went on, 'No one ever gave me nothing, wasn't no
handouts thing, none of that. Work for myself till I get to the
top then no one can answer me for nothing.'

So important was money in his life that he translated even the
closest relationships into financial terms. Being without parents
meant being without handouts, whereas the unconditional love
of a mother he saw as a deluge of generosity impossible to repay.
'You know how you can say to your mum, all those two-pound
meals and dinners you get stacked up for ten, fourteen, seventeen years of your life, you can't afford to pay that back no matter
how long you growin' for.'

He lit the spliff and took a draw. Instead of love, loneliness lay
at the heart of his life. He defined it by the lack of people who
cared enough to give him money. He said, 'Very few people I can
name. Like anything someone's given me, I can actually name an
amount of money they've given me.' Individuals or the state were
all one for him. He went on, 'Even at the job centre I've never
had that much money off one person where I can say, "I don't
even remember how much money you've given me."'

He shook his head and inhaled. He had received so little
love in his life that 'I can afford to pay back anyone who's given
me something' – here his voice turned to disgust – 'apart from

children's home and social services. That's the only persons I can't afford to pay back. But even they treated me like a dickhead so I wouldn't pay them back, you get me? But anyone else you've given me something I can actually go to and say, "Hey that's what you've given me in my life, here, I'm gone." You get me? No one has given me unlimited money where I can say, "I can't remember how much money you've actually given me you know."' He leant forward to fix my tax disc, which had come unstuck. It meant he had no ties of affection: no debts of love. He gestured to the street. 'I can actually leave this area that's how on my own I am. No one ever helped me with shit bruv. You get me? That's the hard life.'

He gave me directions in a protective manner, knowing I was lost without Swagger. Swagger too was busy with the law. He had taken his girlfriend to family court to try and see his son, Tshane. Why not use a mediator? I had asked. Instead they each had a lawyer paid out of legal aid.

Tuggy and I passed a troop of frightening-looking youths. Would I be all right on my own? Tuggy Tug laughed. 'Harry this is my area. This is the block. This is where it goes down. This is where the brains and that come from.' He paused to look fondly at the narrow, steep road and the Victorian houses, their fronts crowded with laurel bushes, dustbins and old bicycles. 'All right, yeah,' he said, 'love this strip. No one goin' to touch you here.'

I was due to pick up Mash. I had insisted he go back to Connexions and he refused to go on his own. I asked Tuggy Tug to join us. He looked at me as if I were three years old. 'I got to eat, Harry,' he said. He had already wasted the morning in court. 'If I don't sell this ting, I don't eat today. Mash, he got a mum, a dad, even uncles man. I got no one to give me a little ten pounds here and there.'

It was the first time he had spoken slightingly of Mash and the first time I realised there was a difference in their backgrounds.

Mash skidded around the garages on an old bike painted pea green. He was breathless and grinned with relief when he spotted me. He had stolen the bike in order to meet me on time. He thought I had 'given up on him' because I had not phoned repeatedly. He had seen my increasingly exasperated calls as a sign of care.

A week earlier I had discovered that Mash had ceased attending football practice. When I asked why, he claimed it was because he had grown out of his football boots. I said I did not believe him. He texted me a photo of the blister on his toe. What about his father or his uncles? He shrugged. They did not care about him enough to take an interest in his football career.

The advisers at the Connexions centre were once again all at lunch. Mash said it made him 'shook' sitting around the centre of Brixton. 'It's a war out there man,' he claimed. 'It stresses me out being here.' I tried to think of a safe place outside Brixton to buy football boots. Peter Jones in Sloane Square was about as safe as it gets, I decided. Surely no one would attack us in Peter Jones. As we drove, he was on the phone to friends about the bike: 'No, get it fam. It's behind the bins. I just need you to watch it a hot minute.' He rang back. The friend had got distracted with something else. Mash rang another friend who could not find it. 'You are not looking.' There was a pause. 'Are you sure you are looking behind the right bin?' So it went on.

Only as we walked through the store's linen department, all gleaming white and tiny blue ribbons, did it occur to me what I was doing. Mash lolloped alongside, hood up, black leather jacket, big jeans slung low, a wolf among the lambs and crystal.

At the escalator he stepped aside to allow three women on. 'Women go first,' he said to me with one of those sudden shafts of politeness or care all the boys displayed and which always undid me. The women looked as if they were up from the country for a day's shopping. They knew about hoodies like Mash. They had just not expected to find one in Peter Jones at the bottom of the escalators. They froze, convinced he planned to mug them from behind. One stepped forward then lost her nerve and stepped back again. 'What good manners you have, Mash,' I exclaimed in order to reassure them. Finally with little rushes and sideways glances at Mash, they fluttered onto the escalator.

In the sports department, the Indian manager tried to ignore Mash and me when I asked him to check Mash's toes. Mash called him 'Boss Man', a term of respect that saw the manager grimace and tell us, with some pleasure, that Peter Jones no longer sold football boots. We found a pair in a nearby sports shop then stopped to eat a steak sandwich. Mash pushed his to one side, embarrassed that his table manners might let him down. He grew quite talkative, head lowered and turned slightly away from me. He was pleased I had made a distinction between Tuggy Tug and him. He said, 'Tuggy Tug's doin' bad things. He will go to jail for sure. The others they don't know where they want to be in five years unlike me. I know where I want to be. I want to have a house and a car and a mortgage. I want to be working.'

I should have enquired how he planned to achieve all this. But his smile disarmed me so I never did ask until far too late.

The sun broke through as we walked along King's Road. I exclaimed how much I was enjoying myself. Mash looked at me, baffled. He was back on the phone about the pea-green bike. One friend had wandered off and he was trying to cajole another to stand guard over the bike. Connexions still looked empty when we passed by.

When I next saw Tuggy Tug, the light and vivacity had left him. It was only two weeks later but the weather had turned cold. We were sitting in the Tickle Me Café watching the rain fall on

Knight's Hill. The café was small, with a counter at the back and a few plastic tables set by a large window overlooking the street. Black-and-white glamour photographs of blondes hung over the fridge – the only decoration. Two bored women stood behind the counter. The service was slow and the food always running out.

Tuggy Tug explained Lambeth Council had not found him a place to stay. Instead they had announced he was Wandsworth's problem. Wandsworth Council wanted a letter from Lambeth confirming this. Meanwhile Tuggy Tug had nowhere to sleep. All he had received by way of help was £10 in Iceland food vouchers. I rang his social worker, another new one, this time a man who announced, 'He's very angry with me at the moment. I am getting an ear bashing and I cherish my ear.' I turned to Tuggy Tug. 'He thinks it's a joke,' I said.

The boys were eating curried goat, the only thing still on the menu. 'Social workers are a joke, fam,' said Tuggy Tug, food restoring some of his old verve. 'They come and go quick like. I've had so many I don't even count no more. The one you just talked to? I've already been told he's only like temporary.'

Bulldog, who had also been in care when not in youth offender institutions, paused from eating. 'It's not a good idea to piss off your social worker. They got the power,' he remarked.

Tuggy Tug resumed: 'If you know someone is not going to be around, no way are you goin' to talk to them. Every time, every time fam, you got to tell them your whole life story.' He shook his head. 'No way am I doin' that again. I tell them, "Read my file. Don't expect me to go all through that shit again."'

Bulldog said, 'They lost me for two years. Didn't see anyone from social services for two years. Then they drop in and make these decisions that change your life and they're off again. Never stay around to ask what you want or see how you do.'

Tuggy Tug leant forward, waving his finger at me over his juice box. 'They got all these boundaries,' he said, drawing out the word. 'That means they just don't care. Boundaries means they get to go home at five o'clock. One time I was in this school play. Fam there were four of us all in care all in this little play. Did one of them social workers like or a foster parents come to that school play? We had nobody. Why? Cos it's out of hours and they don't get no overtime. They should care, man, they should care. I got nothing to eat, no place to stay and what my social worker doin'? Chatting shit.'

Swagger now arrived in a new raincoat of Burberry checks. 'Hello Princess,' he said, a greeting he used on any woman between the ages of fourteen and seventy, 'what are you doin' here?' He glanced through the plate-glass window onto the high street, anxious we should finish and leave. 'You never know who's goin' to come through that door,' he warned.

Shortly afterwards we heard that Tuggy Tug had been arrested and sent to Feltham Young Offenders Institute. I got on the telephone to try and arrange a visit but they refused to tell me if he was even there. 'Mentor!' said the woman as if it were a dirty word. 'I can't give out that kind of information. You are not family or a social worker.' I said he had neither. 'It's for his own protection,' said the woman.

Thirteen

A week later we still had not heard anything from Feltham. I decided to go and see if Tuggy Tug's gang had any news of him and how they were getting on without him.

I parked outside the community centre. The rain was washing down and the meadow was empty of dog walkers. The first gang member I saw was Smalls. He came and sat in my car, tree-trunk legs apart, fists resting on them, his head brushing the roof. Apart from Bulldog, Smalls was the only gang member to have gone to a youth offenders institute. He was worried about what was happening to Tuggy Tug. 'It's violent in there, you get me? They bang you up for twenty-three hours straight. When the youths are coming out of their cells, everyone is kicking off. The fights in there are mash-up man, worse than big-man prison.'

I tried to imagine my son and his friends locked in a cell for twenty-three hours. Had Smalls been afraid? He shook his head. The novelty of three meals a day had seen him fill out and grow five inches in eleven months. 'The staff can punish you and the prisoners can fight you. That is the most that can happen.'

At least he got some education? Smalls said, 'The teachers are scared. The other boys are like me,' he added in case I did not understand. 'The screws are even scared to take us to education. There you are just sitting doing nothing in that hot cell – jail just horrible in summer – it don't make no sense.' In a rare display of emotion, he said, 'I am always miserable in jail.' But then, as usual, he found a good side. 'I tell Tuggy Tug do what other brothers don't do. Pick up a book, don't be peer-pressured. You'll be surprised what you learn.'

What was going to happen to Tuggy Tug? 'I know Tuggy Tug will make money,' Smalls reassured me, but it was difficult to get away from hood thinking. 'When you think negative, things aren't gonna come. It's that simple. Hear me?'

He looked out at the rain, searching for an example to get his point across. 'I've thought about death,' he said finally. 'But once you've made that decision, don't think about death no more. All right you're young, think about living, innit? If it comes, it comes. What will be will be. Hear me? You can die two ways: with sympathy or without it fam.' (With sympathy but no money because you had not robbed or without it because you had stolen from people and they were glad to see you dead.) That was true, I agreed. I had never heard my son or his friends talk about death. I never discussed death with my son as I did with Tuggy Tug and his gang. Death was real and everywhere for them.

Swagger now arrived and we ran into the community centre, where we hoped to find other members of Tuggy Tug's gang. Smalls left, his huge shoulders hunched against the rain. Swagger began to chat to Patricia. Young girls stared at the computers. There were no boys in the centre.

I went outside and found Mash and Bulldog. Mash had on a turquoise cap and heavy black patent leather shoes with a black anorak and jeans. Bulldog was in a grey hoodie, his face in shadow and as usual agitated. I sent Mash into the centre to get out of the rain.

Bulldog said he could not go inside. Being inside the centre made him 'boomy'. Bulldog might be white but he used the Caribbean term for scared. Bulldog was more than scared. He struck me as haunted by perils invisible to the rest of us. We found a corner of the building that gave a little shelter. He rolled a spliff then sucked on it. He was wondering if Tuggy Tug was getting his weed inside and how he was coping. 'I miss that guy, man,' he announced. I said Tuggy Tug was better off without it and told him how drugs affected the teenage brain. Young people who smoked marijuana were twice as likely to develop psychosis and schizophrenia as those who did not. 'Get away!' said Bulldog. 'I never heard that!'

He shook his head. He feared it was too late for him. He had started on drugs and crime as a child. He had been excluded from school at fourteen. By eighteen, he had more than twenty criminal convictions. 'I have been in every kind of trouble there is, GBH, assaulting a policeman.' He pulled his wet hood closer around his face. I had never seen him without the hood up. He went on, 'Right now I am just floating around all over the place. I don't live here. I don't live there. I am homeless, you get me. My mum kicked me out. I don't know where to go most of the time. Tuggy Tug's not around. I don't have nothing to do. I am quite bored with life.' Teenagers say that sort of thing all the time, but rarely with the heartbreaking finality of Bulldog. He glanced away then raised his hand to his face, streaming with rain. He said, 'I am just lost right now.'

At the door of the community centre, I glanced back. The rain was still falling but he had not moved.

Inside I found the atmosphere not much better. Mash was hunched up in a corner. He was on his own without Tuggy Tug or the gang and he hated it. On the other side of the room Patricia demanded to know what he was doing in her centre. She had banned him the year before. Then she accused him of being a baby. 'Oh look, he's going to blabber right now,' she jeered in front of the girls sitting at the computers. I was so shocked I froze. My son would rather I slashed him with a knife than talk to him like that in public.

Mash leapt up and for a moment I thought he would attack Patricia. Instead he ran outside. She followed and there was a sudden explosion of shouting. Mash told her to fuck off. 'You think you are some big woman,' he was yelling, 'but I am never coming back here again.' Swagger, who had been round the corner having a smoke, now joined in. I tried to tell him I had sent Mash into the centre and what Patricia had said; but Swagger was not listening. He said, 'You can't be flying off the handle when you start work.' Mash said that he knew the difference between the workplace and a half-cock social worker like Patricia who he had no respect for. 'She is a nasty woman,' he said.

Swagger just went on shouting at Mash. Finally he stalked off into the rain. I took Mash to the Tickle Me Café to try and calm him down. When we parted, he smiled. 'You can give me a hug now,' he said.

Not long after, the centre closed. Patricia had been using the charity to run a scam. She then disappeared from the area.

I did not hear from the boys for a couple of months. Without Tuggy Tug, we all drifted apart.

Swagger, who was having his own problems, stayed in touch. His solicitor never turned up for his case at the family court. Swagger asked for the case to be postponed but the judge 'was not havin' it'. So Swagger had to represent himself. His girlfriend's solicitor cross-examined him for the better part of a day. His girlfriend did not have to appear in the witness box and her version of events was never questioned. The female judge took her word on everything.

Swagger was ordered not to approach his girlfriend. He repeated to me what he had said in court. 'It's not like I want to see her,' he told the judge. 'I just want to see my son,' he went on, 'what's going to happen to this little man if he does not have his daddy around? He's going to be like one of these boys I am working with right now. He's going to be put out on the road by his mum. He's going to be stabbed up or locked up. I said these little girls lose interest once these boys get big. They can't handle them.'

The judge had remained unimpressed. Swagger was only allowed to see his son in a contact centre for two hours every other week. 'And I got to do one of those anger management courses for nine months,' he said to me. 'For what? What have I done? I never touched her! She's got no doctor's report, no witnesses, nothing. It's doing my head in not seeing my son. It's stressing me out, Harry man.'

It was at this low point that Swagger landed a job with a charity that helped disadvantaged young people. Being Swagger, it was not just any charity. It had rock-star status. I had been to the fund-raising dinner of a similarly successful charity. Bankers with thin blonde wives bid for eco-friendly holidays in Puerto Rico. Just before the bidding began, young people came on stage and described how the charity had transformed their lives. A pop star was so moved that he stood up and donated the royalties from his latest song. A well-known comic urged us to give generously. The goodie bag contained a cashmere hoodie and biscuits baked by appreciative youngsters. Just taking part had left me feeling a better person.

Now Swagger had been hired as a mentor. Here was his big chance. 'Well, it's my effervescent personality, innit,' said Swagger. He glanced down at the tomato-red sweatshirt he was wearing. He looked dazzling. Only close to did you notice the red had run, turning the white stripes on the collar and cuffs pink. Clothes never survived long on Swagger. He always started with such high hopes of every new outfit. When they did not transform his life, he lost interest, giving them away or leaving them scrunched up in the corners of his bedroom. He sighed. 'I need some new clobber,' he said.

The charity asked Swagger to mentor Chantal, an eighteen-year-old girl. The head of the charity was impressed 'by my people skills', he said. He accompanied Chantal on a weekend course where she suddenly turned violent and threw a computer at a girl. As a child, her stepfather had sexually abused her. She reacted badly to laughter because his women used to laugh at her while it was going on. That sounded serious. Had they given him any training or advice? He shook his head. I wondered at the wisdom of putting a vulnerable young girl and Swagger with his looks and charm so close together. Even Swagger was nervous. He asked his mother and me for tips on childcare. He had no idea how to help Chantal. In the end he bought her a bottle of perfume.

The job was having a miraculous effect on his domestic life. Despite their court battle, Swagger's girlfriend allowed him to move back home. She was delighted he was finally in work. Every morning before leaving for the charity, Swagger got Tshane up, changed his nappy and gave him breakfast. 'I got this little routine goin',' he announced proudly.

Over the next few weeks Swagger began to grumble about the staff. He felt he was being used for his 'life skills' and not appreciated for much else. I got impatient with him. He should be listening and learning and above all grateful they had given him a job. Look what had happened, I said: he was back with his girlfriend and Tshane. At any moment she could report him to the police. He was not meant to approach his girlfriend or child – never mind live with them. Swagger looked miserable. Nonetheless he urged me to come to the centre run by the charity and see for myself.

In an article the head of the charity described how about 500 young people used the centre a week, fifty or sixty turning up every day for a nutritious meal, education and Pilates. Apart from Pilates, this sounded exactly what Tuggy Tug and his gang needed. The centre was indeed homely, with shelves of books and the smell of cooking. Instead of fifty or sixty young people, however, there was just one sulky teenager over whom ten staff hovered.

'See,' said Swagger. Charities took on Swagger because he was black and an ex-con. But his upbringing meant he was no ordinary ex-con. His father had worked with young people. Swagger knew how things should be done. He had a diamond-hard view on how young people should be treated. He was unable to compromise – even when it put his own happiness in jeopardy. 'Come down again on a Friday,' he urged me.

On the Friday about twenty young people were having lunch, with more coming and going. One nineteen-year-old girl had brought her baby. She had put herself into care at the age of twelve and started visiting the centre a few years later. 'It was good then,' she explained. 'You had respect for the place. We got paid for jobs and same if we studied. Now the system has collapsed. You get money every week without doing no jobs and no education.'

I sat down at another table and asked the young people there why they came. They looked surprised. 'For the money, of course,' one young man explained. Every Friday the staff handed out cash in envelopes ranging from £50 to £200. This is a serious amount to a young person receiving roughly £50 a week from the state. The allowance appeared to be the key to the popularity of the centre. 'You don't see most of the kids coming any other day,' admitted one member of staff. Many young people agreed. As one said, 'I come on Friday lunchtimes to socialise, pick up my allowance then I go.' The young people I spoke to resented the fact that some got more than others. They accused the head of the charity of favouritism.

Two care leavers, sent by the Prince's Trust for a week's course, dismissed the centre as 'chaotic'. They complained that no one gave them credit for their hard work. 'The bad kids go unpunished,' they sighed. One care leaver added, 'Everything gets stolen. I can't go to the loo without carrying all my things with me.'

During their visit, a young man had turned up furious that his money had been cut. He threatened staff, shouted abuse then snatched up a fire extinguisher and threw it into the office where the woman who handed out the cash crouched, terrified. He insisted on telephoning the head of the charity, who immediately overruled the decision taken by staff and restored the young man's allowance.

It turned out Bulldog had started going to the charity at fifteen. Two years later he was a crack addict. He had gone there hopeful of getting some kind of education but he did not learn anything. He just picked up money every week, which he spent on his addiction. 'I am not going back there,' he said. 'If you stay you don't progress none, do you get me? You got to leave to progress.'

Swagger was bitter. He said, 'What do they think addicts are going to spend that money on? The charity knows this but those handouts brings in the bodies and it's the numbers of bodies that bring in next year's funding.'

Outside I saw four or five cars queuing up. Young people jumped out of them and ran into the community centre. They returned a few moments later, waving their envelopes in the air and grinning. Then they got back into the car and were driven away.

Nearby I found the manager of the community centre in a coffee shop with another member of staff. I asked about the money. She looked uncomfortable. 'Well it keeps them off the street,' she said.

A few months later I heard the charity had received a large

grant from the government. The news generated heart-warming publicity. I was confused. Had my visit been a one-off? Maybe things had changed since then? Even so, the gulf between the reports and what I had seen and heard took my breath away. Swagger shrugged. 'Who's goin' to ask us, crack addicts, bank robbers, street kids, kids from care, our views? Who's goin' to talk to us, take our word when all those nice middle-class people are saying how wonderful they are?'

He was sacked shortly after for doing drugs with the girl he was looking after. 'I was trying to show her you can take it or leave it,' he said indignantly. 'She hasn't had none since!' he added. The result was predictable. His girlfriend kicked him out and 'locked down on my son'. Once again he was deprived of any chance to see Tshane.

Fourteen

After that I did not hear anything from Swagger or the gang until late December. By then Tuggy Tug had been in Feltham for three months. Just before Christmas Swagger rang.

He had bumped into Bulldog. 'He's a bit down without Tuggy Tug and I am also on account of not seeing Tshane,' he explained. 'So I'm saying let's go over the waters and visit Harry.' I took them to a restaurant in Camden Town.

The reason for Bulldog's gloom soon became clear. He was on the run from the police. He had spent the last two Christmases inside on charges of grievous bodily harm. He was determined to spend this holiday out of jail. When the police came around with a warrant for his arrest – on this occasion for biting the nose of a bouncer at a club in Hastings – 'I had to jump out of the back door in my boxers, hopping fences and all that. As soon as Christmas is past, I will hand myself in.'

The waiter ignored us and was abrupt when I pulled him over despite the fact that it was a Caribbean restaurant and Swagger was the only Caribbean in the place. Swagger shook his head at my anger. 'She needs to do one of those courses we done in prison,' he said to Bulldog, 'I'm always telling her,' and they both laughed. Bulldog smiled at me and pulled down his hood. It was the first time I had seen him without it around his face and head. He had a broken nose, a crew cut and a hairline that came low and tight over his forehead like a band. Swagger ordered them both Jack Daniel's. 'Ask him for ketchup,' he said to me, 'I need ketchup with my tilapia.'

I questioned Bulldog about his childhood. He was the most troubled and unpredictable of the gang. Tuggy Tug had told me he remembered nothing until the age of five and his arrival at his elderly black foster mother's house. He had no memories of his real mother, who was a crack addict. Bulldog's mother also took crack and he remembered her only too well. His earliest memories were of pain. 'Too much happen to me when I was little. When good things come my way, I don't trust them.'

As a child he was thrown around and hit. At the age of four he watched his stepfather batter his mother with a rolling pin: 'I saw her blood spatter.' It was the little boy who called the police. His stepfather was jailed for attempted murder. Two years later when he was released, social services told Bulldog's mother she could not have the stepfather live in the same house as Bulldog. She had to choose between them. She chose her husband and Bulldog was taken into care.

He had entered a system that is failing on a catastrophic scale. Of the 6,000 young people who leave care every year, 4,500 of them will leave with no educational qualifications whatsoever. Within two years of leaving care 3,000 will be unemployed, 1,200 will be homeless. Only 60 will make it to university. It is not for lack of money. The government spends about £60,000 a year on each child in care – double what it costs to send a child to Eton.

It is not just a tragedy for individuals like Bulldog and Tuggy Tug. As I discovered when I researched my think-tank report on the subject, a successful care system would transform this country. At a stroke, it would empty a third of our prisons and shift half of all prisoners under the age of twenty-five out of the criminal justice system. It would halve the number of prostitutes, reduce by between a third and a half the number of homeless and remove 80 per cent of *Big Issue* sellers from our street corners.

Not only is our system failing young people like Bulldog and Tuggy Tug, it is failing society and perpetuating an underclass.

Bulldog quickly learnt that there was little difference between the care system and his home life. Both were chaotic and dangerous for a small boy.

'It was violent in the children's home,' he said. 'They are supposed to take care of you, you get me, but they don't give a shit. At the end of the day they go home. We don't. Kids have to grow up fast, learn the street. It's a bad environment. That's why we are going to grow up a bum. We get brought up violent, get me, rape and shit like that. You get abused, sick shit like that. We get a different attitude towards life because of the way we been treated. They should have better social workers, at the end of the day.'

He found himself moved from care home to foster parents then back again. 'They don't like you in one place. I don't know why. Two months, all going nice, you happy, you trust your social worker and then it's just up and go. If you stay in a community, grow up in one place, you would turn out a nice chap, you get me, cos you would get that love. If I had stayed in one place I would have a job,' his eyes widened, 'I might even have a car.' He shook his head. 'Kids need love. No one can tell me different. You want love from your mum and dad. There is no one to care if we live or die. That's why we go on as we go on because our family don't love us. If you don't have that love you turn out different. There's no two ways about it. My mum' – he paused – 'she's a bit twisted and messed up.'

'I started smoking weed at seven so bad business at the end of the day.' By nine he was staying away from the home for days at a time. At the age of ten, he moved into a ticket box in Waterloo station for the warmth. He used the public toilets to wash. 'I didn't live like no tramp.' He stole to eat. 'We robbed for food because we don't get no food anyway in the home.' It got snatched by the bigger children. 'You have to do it for yourself.'

He would be away four or five days before the staff in the home reported him as missing to the police. When the police returned him, the staff shrugged. 'Back, are you?' they remarked. As Bulldog said, 'They don't give a shit.' In the children's home they let him smoke weed and take girls to his room. He looked on this licence as a sign of laziness and indifference. 'They just sit in their office chatting shit about how bad we were. They didn't care. You know if there is a caring person. A caring person is on your case. When someone cares and you don't listen and walk away, you feel bad inside. But you know they care.'

At twelve he mugged someone for £1.

He leant forward. 'You don't know one kid in care who done well. You lose contact. You been moved about all the time. You don't make that many friends.'

He rubbed his forehead as if his hairline were pulled too tight. 'You can't trust social workers, counsellors. They stab you in the back. They just pass the buck on. They think you all bad, all disturbed. That's how they see us. They go, "Oh it's too late, you are going to end in jail."'

What would he do instead? 'If I was a social worker? I would do things different. I would find out the kid's problems and help him with that. If you are put in charge of a kid, at least know his fucking problem and his history. It's good money for social workers,' he said. 'They still get paid at the end of the month. Another kid, another problem that's all it is. They just jog you on at the end of the day. They forget about us. I get frustrated. They don't keep a check on you to see if you are doing well later on; what has happened to you; if you have a normal life. They just see you as another case.'

Sometimes he sneaked into people's homes at night. He did not take anything. He just wanted to sit and imagine what it was like to be part of a family, to live in a home, to go to school, to be ordinary. With the family upstairs asleep he would bounce on the sofas, walk through to the kitchen, stand there, the silence gathering around him, then slip out the way he had climbed in.

All the moves meant he had attended school for just two years. He could not read or write and we had to read the menu to him.

I ordered pudding. Swagger and Bulldog ordered more Jack Daniel's. Bulldog lowered his head and began to sway, the drink making him sad. 'Bad things I done for money,' he admitted. 'You have to do them things to live.' When he robbed he used a knife: 'I wouldn't care if I stabbed or not.' Swagger and I both started.

Bulldog just looked at us. 'It's true man. I been brought up differently. I am not getting that love and affection. If you see a lot of evil, you turn evil. If you see good, you turn good.' He glanced downwards and fiddled with his spoon. 'It's making me sound bad,' he admitted. 'I would rather rob a man who would hurt me back.' He shook his head and sighed. 'I didn't want this life. It just happened.'

Afterwards we went roller-skating in a disco. Camden was another area of London that Swagger knew well. During his childhood, his father had a stall in Camden Lock most week-ends. The guards frisked Swagger and Bulldog but waved me past. Twenty minutes later I found myself creeping along the edge of a skating rink that wound its way through a series of vast rooms. Swagger and Bulldog had long since joined the crowds of skaters that swished past me. In the centre of the floor the best skaters, mostly young black men, danced and leapt, their skin licked by the swirling lights. Suddenly in front of me Bulldog twisted to a halt. 'You never done roller-skating?' he asked in amazement. I shook my head. He smiled and took my hands. 'Easy, easy,' he encouraged. Swagger, who had been half dancing, half flirting at the centre, sped over. Together they pulled me at speed through the skaters, lights and music breaking over our heads.

Later I found myself outside sitting on a step with Bulldog. A thin shard of a moon had climbed over the warehouse and cobbled street in front of us. At sixteen, disgusted with the state, Bulldog had signed himself out of care. 'I went back to Mum but she was on the mad side. She was a crack addict. I shouldn't talk about this shit but she didn't love me.' She encouraged him to take crack, 'and I didn't want to disappoint her'.

He mused, 'If I lived in a posh area and had a family would I be on drugs? I wouldn't do heavy drugs because I wouldn't be so down. That's why kids like me do crack. It takes the problems away for a couple of hours. But at the end of the day, problems don't go away. You get me? At the end of the day the past always comes back to us. You can't get away. The past is in us.'

I promised to visit him in prison. He saw my distress. 'Easy, easy,' he said gently. I tried to reconcile the violent crack addict I knew Bulldog to be with the young man next to me. I tried but failed.

Fifteen

In January Tuggy Tug finally came out of Feltham. It was very cold, the canal near my house frozen over. At Swagger's suggestion we took Tuggy Tug, Smalls and Lips to eat pancakes in a restaurant on the top floor of John Lewis. His mother used to treat Swagger there when he was little. I feared Tuggy Tug had gone beyond pancakes but the expedition proved a success.

First we looked at the wide-screen TVs and compared prices, an occupation all the boys enjoyed. Then they ate pasta followed by pancakes with Maltesers, chocolate sauce and ice cream. Far from the hardened criminal who I thought might emerge from prison, Tuggy Tug pressed his stack of pancakes like a child and asked me to admire how it oozed chocolate. 'This is my first restaurant meal of the new year and it tastes boom [good],' he declared.

He did not have much to say on the subject of Feltham. The present and its problems consumed him. He announced he was no longer 'running' with Mash. Mash had proved 'a snake'. In Tuggy Tug's absence, Mash had taken over his links. In other words he had seized his supply and distribution network. Far from concentrating on his football, Mash was now a drug dealer. This was news to me. Tuggy Tug said that was not all. Mash had failed to include them in a job to strip the copper tiles off the roof of the boarded-up community centre. It had been a big job and on their block. Tuggy Tug was furious.

Smalls leant forward to explain how the job was done. 'You

cut each tile with shears then roll it up, pulling out the nails as you go.' Mash and another boy had worked on the roof, throwing the tiles down to two men below who picked them up and put them in a van. Mash had hogged the job. First he did not tell them it was happening. 'Mash only told us right at the end when the Feds were already circulatin' around in a helicopter,' said Tuggy Tug, waving his spoon in the air with disgust. Then Mash told them they needed to bring their own special shears. Tuggy Tug went on, 'But we saw he was using no special shears. He was using plain, ordinary garden shears.' The boys all leant forward in their consternation. The men had sold the tiles to a scrap merchant for £7,000. A number of people on the estate had congratulated them. Tuggy Tug and the others had missed out on the money and the acclaim.

I told Tuggy Tug he should at all costs no longer be involved in things like that. He did not take my comment quite as I had intended. 'I never slip,' he assured me. 'You would never catch me slipping bruv. You have to run up in my hostel and kick through bare doors just to catch the real G's bed.' He saw my puzzlement and elaborated on the precautions he took to keep safe. 'See once I leave my door, either a taxi's there or one of the dons [members of his gang] and that's how a man's moving, man. I would never get on a bus. See where you picked me up from? You would never see me on a bus.' I had walked past a minicab rank and been surprised to discover that far from shunning Tuggy Tug and his gang, they shouted out greetings. He even had a favourite driver.

I asked him if he was carrying a weapon. 'No cos I knew I was coming to see you lot.'

But would he normally?

'Yeah most definitely,' replied Tuggy Tug. He went on, 'Not to hurt no one, not to go out there and use it intentionally. But just to hold my corner. And I will hurt someone if someone tried to come to me. Yeah, that's the reason. That's not a game bruv. That's man's life bruv . . . all the surrounding shit and that.' Feltham had altered things. Tuggy Tug explained, 'I'm a big man now bruv.'

Tuggy Tug's time in Feltham did not lessen my desire to change his life, difficult as that task increasingly seemed. Besides, I enjoyed our expeditions. When I crossed Vauxhall Bridge, the glass and steel buildings on either side seemed like a guardian mountain range to another world. As I slipped into the shadow of the tunnel beyond, I started to get excited. I never knew what was going to happen – and with Tuggy Tug something always happened.

At the same time I knew Tuggy Tug spoke the truth. He was turning into a man – at least as far as the criminal justice system was concerned. For my son that meant leaving home and going to university. Growing up for Tuggy Tug meant big man's prison. That was the next milestone. I still had not accepted the inevitability of his life. I still thought I could win.

My weapon on this occasion was the Tate Modern. None of the boys had ever been to an art gallery. Once again I had failed, despite much talk of the gallery's diversity strategy, to get any help or information on how to interest a South London gang in modern art. Tuggy Tug soon made clear what grabbed his attention – the prices. When I told him how much a Picasso was worth, he exclaimed, 'I am up for a career change!' We then had to rank each painting in the room according to value. Tuggy Tug rushed between a Picasso and a Klein trying to work out why one was worth more than another. I did not have an answer. I talked vaguely of colour and form but convinced neither of us.

Smalls joined me in front of a Rothko and listened politely to my explanation. All the time his eyes flicked to the girls standing in clusters in front of the paintings. None of them had seen girls like these before. I remarked that art galleries were popular with girls and the boys looked around with new interest.

Smalls moved in on one group of girls, followed by the others. At first the girls responded, combing their hair with their fingers before tossing it back. Then I watched their faces freeze as they realised these young men were not playing at the street. They were the real thing. Subtly, trying not to cause offence, they scattered like a flock of peahens. The boys returned to report back.

How had they got on? Tuggy Tug said, 'We are more used to our girls. We just have two completely different styles.'

Lips agreed: 'They're nothing compared to our girls.'

Were they well spoken? 'They got their boring questions,' said Smalls.

Did they say anything interesting? 'Na, they didn't really say nothing good.'

So were they stuck up? Smalls considered. 'If you really wanted to talk to them, be friends or whatever, you got to, yeah . . .'

'Step your game up,' decided Lips.

We had lunch looking out over St Paul's, the Thames jolting with wind and sunlight. Tuggy mused on the madness of people who spent millions on a painting. So what would he buy when he succeeded? Lips nodded. 'What are you gonna spend it on? What bitches? What champagne are you gonna drink bruv?'

Tuggy Tug grinned like a ten-year-old at the prospect. But he did not expect to change. 'See when you live hood shit and you do everything hood,' he explained, 'what all you white people say, yeah, is that we shine for [what interests us] is jewellery, guns, knives, cars, chains. We grind on the road because that's what we enjoy. That's our hobbies, innit?'

He was warming to his argument and we all watched, fascinated. 'What does white people enjoy? . . . Golf. Or swimming pools in the back of their houses. See them white people they spend millions of pounds on golf courses. Golf you know! What they don't shine into the light is why they spend millions of pounds on just grass and a hole. And that can house a million African people.' Tuggy Tug's brain immediately calculated the finances of this conceit. 'And if they house a million African people on this one golf course, there's a million African people who work for you for free for a year for ten pounds a week.

'The things we enjoy is different cos that's what we been brought up around. They been around and seen that golf shit and' – he searched for examples – 'Harvard and boats. You think it's a joke? Trust me bruv,' he said to the others, 'Harry took me to the river. You remember that man in Richmond?' he said to me of someone we had met restoring his boat. 'They spend millions of pounds on little canoes and shit. Painting up rusty boats.' He put on a prissy voice to take off the man. We were all laughing now.

But what did he want out of life? I asked. 'To tell the God's honest truth, I just want some money blud. I would just like a nice stable income. That is what I like.'

Lips said, 'But a man's got to live lavish blud.'

Tuggy Tug shook his head. 'Most people say houses, cars. I just want a good income. Stuff like . . .' – his eyes widened as another idea opened up – 'yes nice . . . real estate.'

Smalls said with his usual perception, 'You gotta do what most guys don't do.'

'Real estate,' said Tuggy Tug.

'What?' Lips scooped up his last bit of ice cream.

'Real estate, that's what you got to invest in,' stated Tuggy Tug as the others gazed at him, barely catching up with this new idea. 'Buy two new houses and then you're caked. That's it, all I want is just two houses, a nice car and at least ten bags spending money man, that's a stable income, and a fucking Benz.' He suddenly looked ashamed. It was the first time he had sworn in front of me.

'That's light work,' said Lips with admiration.

'That's light work? I would never lift a finger again. I would kick back.' Tuggy Tug sighed with satisfaction at his plan. 'Yeah I'll go grey [grow old] off two houses. I got clipped toenails and just drive my Benz to the houses every week and get eight bills [one bill = £100] a month off both houses. Sixteen hundred a month.' He looked at the others. 'You don't know no one who's making that blud. Sixteen hundred a month.' Another benefit occurred to him. 'Roughly legit,' he added, 'you can't get nicked for that.'

Afterwards we walked by the river. Tuggy Tug suddenly said, 'Fam, look at that building.' Pleased they were developing an aesthetic appreciation, I turned to where he was pointing. The building had copper dripping down the sides like icing on a cake. They exclaimed with delight and discussed returning with garden shears. 'Copper's on the table, Harry,' said Tuggy Tug. (Copper is easy to sell because of the demand in the market for metals.)

A few days later I turned up on the estate to find Tuggy Tug chatting to a girl who he introduced as a friend of his. Dimples was mixed-race and flashily dressed in black boots, tight pants and a brown leather jacket with a brown hoodie beneath. Her hair was drawn back into a ponytail and she wore huge gold hoop earrings decorated with orange and turquoise stones and one large turquoise stone set in each lobe. She was eighteen and had a son of three. I was intrigued. Here was the female equivalent of Tuggy Tug, a female member of his gang and the mother of future Tuggy Tugs. When Swagger and Tuggy Tug left to meet the others, I invited her to the Tickle Me Café for some carrot cake.

Dimples's son had not enjoyed an auspicious start. Dimples had been fifteen years old, pregnant and up in court on a charge of grievous bodily harm and shoplifting. She remarked, 'I smoked so much weed, I thought I was going to lose my baby.'

What about abortion, I asked, had she considered that? She reacted angrily: 'I don't want to be called no cemetery belly,' she said. She was thinking of putting him into care but Tuggy Tug and Smalls begged her to keep the child. 'I said to them, "I can't do this on my own. You need to be here." And they have. They have been here straight.' She paused then added, 'They do have a heart. You just don't see it.'

When Sure Start failed to pay her the £500 all teenage mothers are supposed to receive, Tuggy Tug bought her a buggy, and Smalls a cot. Tuggy Tug 'even chose my baby's name'. As for the baby's father, 'They sorted him out and beat him up for not helping.' She dismissed his behaviour as 'damn disgusting. You wanted to be close and have sex now you don't want to know me.'

I asked about the violence. She said at fifteen she had been part of a girl gang. She did not think of herself as in a gang. It was more like a group of girls who hung around together and backed each other up.

She described the first time she acted as gang leader. 'We got a call one evening. One of our friends had been assaulted and she was on her own. "Come down," she urged.' She had started at a sixth-form college where 'some people had issues with her'. Dimples and her friends caught a bus to the college and tracked down the girl who had assaulted their friend. 'We weren't havin' it.'

Dimples remembered the moment before she attacked. She had not been drinking or taking drugs; but the other girls were jeering and urging her on. She said, 'You want to look big in front of people. The main reason I hit her was to look big in front of my girls. I hit her in her head, grabbed her down, got her on the floor then punched her and stamped her on her face.'

That was the first of many such episodes. Dimples explained, 'When you are in a gang it's hard to say no to someone because you don't want to look like an idiot. There are certain things you can't say no to.' She and her friends, about ten teenage girls, ambushed professional women returning from an evening out, stealing money and jewellery.

Dimples admitted that of course she liked the money but it was the violence that attracted her. 'I did enjoy it. At primary school, I fought boys. I knew I could take them on. Honestly I did not care if I got beaten up or not. I am just not scared. You think you are untouchable, that you won't get caught. So nothing is going to stop you,' She paused a moment. 'I wanted respect and it gives you this power. I knew what I was doing.'

The violence discharged her anger. 'I felt calm afterwards. I would light a fag and feel, you know, really good.'

In the two years I had known Tuggy Tug and his gang, not once had they mentioned the violence that played such a part in their lives. Dimples, being a girl, shared every detail. She moved closer and lowered her voice, seeking comfort and affection even as she described the assault that had landed her in prison.

Dimples had been out with about four from her gang when they passed another girl in the street. She was pretty, well dressed and glanced at them, they decided, with disdain.

Dimples described what happened next. 'So I just beat her up. She tried to run. I punched her in the face. My friend held her and I punched her some more. She fell to the ground in like a second and me and my friend we proper beat her up. I stamped on her. The others ran away. We went on punching and kicking her.' She paused. 'You think she was not that injured. Really we thought that.' But the girl was in fact badly hurt. Four weeks later the police arrived at her door and arrested her. 'I got GBH. It was not worth it in the end.'

'Afterwards I wondered why did I do it? What made me so angry?' One of the reasons she had got pregnant was 'to sort myself out and put a stop to all that madness'. The other reason was that she did not like living with her mother, herself a single mother.

What about her father? She said, 'I do know my father but he's got a lot of other kids. He gave me a little twenty pounds here and there but he was never there for me.' She was desperate for anything that felt like love. 'I would not have needed to go out looking for someone if my dad had loved me.' Not having a father's affection made it hard for her to turn down demands for sex. 'I thought I had to be accepted so I slept with them. When a boy wanted me, it made me feel special. Oh my gosh, it became a really big thing.'

Like Tuggy Tug, school had not helped her to a better life. Only 12 per cent of pupils at her school had got five good GCSEs. 'My time in school was crap. I didn't learn anything. The teachers were simply there for the money. They were not bothered if I learnt or not.' In the absence of any qualifications, where Tuggy Tug and his friends took to crime, she got pregnant.

What about marriage? Dimples looked downcast. 'I would love to get married,' she admitted, 'but I am not in the marrying crowd.' None of the young men she knew had jobs, 'They are on the road, doing their ting, or banged up.' She paused to inspect her nails, each one decorated with a pink crystal, then touched her hair which was slick with gel. 'None of the girls around here get married. We just have kids.'

What about having a baby so young? 'They tell you a baby mashes up your life,' she said. 'But I didn't have a life to mash up.' Apart from appearing in court for GBH, 'I wasn't doing a lot else at the time.'

Had a baby improved her life? Here Dimples's face lit up. 'Definitely,' she said. It gave her everything she had lacked before. Having a baby was the only way she could achieve an independent adult existence. First she got somewhere to live, which meant she could leave home and 'get out of that situation with my mum's drug taking'. Then the baby had transformed her finances. 'I'm actually claiming benefits. My living situation is a hundred times better.' And it had put right 'the madness' of her upbringing. 'I had a really, really bad childhood. I just thought a baby would give me that stability and also give me something that follows you around all day telling you they love you.' Her reasons for motherhood, I noticed, were all about herself. She had not mentioned her little boy.

I thought of Tuggy Tug's childhood and wondered how long her euphoria would last. How long before she inflicted on her child all the problems that had blighted her own upbringing? The facts are cruel and inescapable. Teenage mothers are three times more likely to suffer poor mental health than other mothers. Babies born to teenage mothers are 60 per cent more likely to die in their first year than those born to other parents. Mothers of children on the 'at risk' register are five times more likely to be single teenage mothers. Like their mothers before them, they will have boyfriends who are a danger to their children. The Children's Society reports that 25 per cent of all youngsters living in stepfamilies run away before the age of sixteen. Many are younger than eleven. We have created a generation of young women like Dimples whose only chance of independence is to become a single mother and to produce future Tuggy Tugs.

Swagger now arrived in the café and Dimples said she had to pick up her son from nursery school. I wanted to see Tuggy Tug and the boys but Swagger did not think that was a good idea. He had just come from a flat on the estate belonging to the mother of one of the boys. He had left Tuggy Tug, Lips and Jiggers sitting around the kitchen table with a tin of Celebration chocolates. That sounded innocuous enough. Swagger shook his head. Instead of chocolates, the tin was filled with skunk. The boys were packing the weed into small, clear plastic bags ready for distribution. Swagger reported Tuggy Tug was elated. 'Mash tried to chop off my legs when I was inside,' he had said. 'But now I am at full throttle. Full throttle fam. Mash has lost his line [customers] because I am back.'

I asked what that meant. Swagger explained Tuggy Tug was not just dealing, he had gone on to the next stage. He now had younger boys distributing for him as well. 'My weed is in the schools fam,' he had exclaimed delightedly to Swagger in the kitchen.

I was horrified. 'I have to get him a job,' I said. 'This has got to stop.' Swagger shook his head. Who was going to employ Tuggy Tug? Despite his brightness, energy and ambition, he could barely read and write. What job, even if he got one, could match what he made from drugs? What unskilled work could provide the excitement and satisfaction of being his own boss? 'It's all about the cheddar [money], Harry,' said Swagger. While Tuggy Tug did not see the point of changing, there was not much I or anyone could do.

To cheer me up, Swagger suggested we visit Bulldog, who was out on remand. He had moved back with his mother and wanted to see us.

Swagger used my phone to get directions from Bulldog. Neither he nor the boys ever used maps. 'Turn here, do a right.' He listened. 'A left and yeah, we're stopping here.' We parked outside a small Victorian house. In the next-door garden, the red flowers on a large, shambling camellia bush were turning brown and rotting on the ground.

We rang the front-door bell. Inside screams suddenly erupted. We heard a smash and a thud. Swagger was pulling me back when Bulldog threw open the door. I caught a glimpse of bare boards, walls covered in filth and a huge TV screen. Hatred like wind gusted out at us.

A white woman screamed, 'Come on cunt. Get my fucking machete or get the fuck out of here.' Bulldog was trying to stand between his mother and us. Swagger pulled at my arm but I could not move. Bulldog turned back inside. 'Yeah Mum, I'll get it,' he shouted with equal violence, 'I'll get your fucking machete.' 'Then fucking get it,' she screamed at him. He looked at us, his face suddenly that of a panic-stricken child. 'Not a good time,' he said and closed the door.

Swagger got me down the path and into the car. 'That is the kind of violence in them families,' he said. 'He tries to be detached but that's his mum innit? That house must be worth three hundred bags,' he added as we drove away.

Sixteen

After the kitchen incident, I almost gave up on Tuggy Tug. My relationship with him had always been a balancing act between my affection for him and knowledge of his criminality. Now the criminal was taking over. He was dealing on a large scale. I tried to talk to him about it but what was there to say? Tuggy Tug appeared set on a criminal career. We both knew I had nothing to offer in its place. For almost a month I did not see him or chat to him on the phone. I missed our expeditions and worried what was happening to him. Then in February, Tuggy Tug and I received an invitation to a lunch that was to change everything.

It did not start off promisingly. Bobby Cummines, our host, had been one of the UK's most dangerous criminals and an associate of both the Krays and the Richardsons.

In 1988 Bobby emerged from prison after a thirteen-year sentence for armed robbery determined never to return. He stacked shelves in Tesco, got a degree, went into property and became an adviser to the government on prison reform. He started a charity for ex-offenders called Unlock and received an OBE for his charitable work. Now he was about to appear in a TV documentary. In November the previous year I had written about Tuggy Tug and his gang for the *Sunday Times*. Bobby's PR, hopeful for some publicity, invited Tuggy Tug, Swagger and me to the Liberal Club in Whitehall where Bobby was a member.

Neither Swagger nor I could possibly foresee the effect of this lunch on our own budding gangster, Tuggy Tug.

Swagger was reluctant to come but not for the reasons I had anticipated. 'People going to ask what right have I? "Do you think you are some sort of gangsta then?"' I agreed it did seem the qualification for an invite. I pointed out he had done six years for robbery. The criminal justice system obviously considered him a gangster and so he cheered up.

The Liberal Club required a suit. Swagger had any number of designer jackets which he wore with jeans. Finally he remembered a pair of black trousers he had bought for the odd catering job. That still left the problem of shoes. He owned trainers in every design and colour but not a single pair of 'big man's shoes'.

My challenge was to find Tuggy Tug a suit then persuade him to put it on. In the end I borrowed one of my son's. Now he was in the sixth form, my son had to wear one for school. I also took a shirt and tie my mother had given him for Christmas.

The next problem was getting there on time. I left four hours to drive to Brixton, pick up Swagger, track down Tuggy Tug, get him ready and then drive to Whitehall and find a parking space.

Tuggy Tug was not 'on the road' as I had feared but waiting for us in his room. Even more unusually, he called us. We called back. Where were we? he demanded. Swagger shouted down my mobile, 'We will tell them who are the real gangstas, who is on the grind right now!' Tuggy Tug interrupted. He needed Swagger to bring him a toothbrush, toothpaste and deodorant.

Tuggy Tug was living in a hostel, the fourth I had visited. It is difficult to understand a so-called hoodie without seeing the places many of them call home. Tuggy Tug's room was small with a narrow bed, no blanket, a cupboard and a view over a strip of rubbish-filled garden. His clothes were in two bin bags on the bed. His neighbours were other single men: drug dealers, addicts, ex-cons, alcoholics – a number of them suffering from mental health problems.

I had framed a photograph taken of him beneath the giant guns outside the Imperial War Museum. He was delighted. Apart from his mobile phones, his clothes and a small portable TV, it turned out to be his only possession and his only photograph. He had no photographs of his childhood or his family.

He placed it on top of the cupboard. 'I can lie in bed and look at it; take in the big guns,' he said. He showed a rare moment of introspection. 'That was a good day. That was before I went to prison.'

'How long have we been seeing you then?' wondered Swagger.

Tuggy Tug began to work it out. Other teenagers mark the passing of time by celebrations, achievements and what they are doing at school. None of these applied to Tuggy Tug. In their absence he determined his past in two ways: how much he had been earning and what punishment he had been on.

'When I met Harry I was younger and a bit stupid then and doing dumb shit, I was on a tenner, twenty pound, five pound, that's how young I was, you get me?' He paused to consider. 'So it was before my ASBO got put on. And my ASBO's almost done and I've been on this for about two years. I've known her for like a year before that. So I've known Harry for almost three years comin' on. Isn't it man?' He gave a big smile and flicked his hand at me. 'Yeah so Harry come down here and jam with me for like three years.'

He exclaimed over my son's suit. Far from being reluctant, he was so eager to try the clothes. He pulled on the trousers without pausing to take off his tracksuit bottoms. When I remonstrated, he explained, 'I get cold!' He was so thin, the trousers fitted. He took off his hoodie, used the deodorant, then carefully, as if the fabric might rub away beneath his fingers, put on my son's shirt. He watched himself button it up in the mirror. 'Ra, ra, ra,' he shouted at us.

He raised the collar and turned to me. I hung the tie around his neck but he shook his head. He had never put on a tie before. I fumbled at it, tying the knot too fatly, aware of the last time I had done this for someone – my son, equally excited, then aged five and starting school.

As Tuggy Tug put on each piece of clothing, he sung out in delight, 'Swagger, Swagger, Swagger.' I thought, I have organised this but it is Swagger who is the grown-up man in his life. It is Swagger whom he loves.

I held out a pair of my son's shoes, barely worn before he grew out of them. Even so, at size 9, they were far too large for Tuggy Tug, who was a size 5½. I glanced at his trainers lined up beneath the window. Tiny and with their flourish of brightly coloured laces, they looked as if they belonged to a child.

We shrugged him into the jacket. He could barely contain himself, posing this way and that in front of the mirror. 'I never been as smart as this – not even for court,' he declared.

He then brushed his teeth but his mouth flooded with blood. He did not know about dental floss or gum disease. He had never been to a dentist. As a child in care you could refuse to go. 'Human rights,' he said vaguely.

When I looked into it, I discovered that once again Tuggy Tug was correct. A note to the annual statistics published by the Department for Education and Skills on children in care explains: 'It must be borne in mind', it urges those 'considering' why a quarter of children in care fail to visit a dentist, 'that children have a right to refuse a health assessment or dental check.' But for Tuggy Tug's panic at his blood-filled mouth, I might have skimmed over that note. Instead for me it now summed up all that is wrong with our care system. Gum disease should not be a right. Forcing a child to go to the dentist shows you care. Giving children the right not to go is an excuse to shrug off a difficult task and abandon responsibility. Young people like Tuggy Tug and Bulldog knew they were allowed to do what they liked because no one cared enough to stop them.

Tuggy Tug was admiring himself in the mirror and calling out to Swagger. 'All I need is a comb and some cream and I am gone clear,' he announced, accusing Swagger in his blue jacket and collarless shirt of being 'butters' – ugly.

As we walked down the stairs, the manager of the hostel and his wife came out to check us. They were large, unhealthy-looking and spoke with a South African accent. The wife wore a baggy white T-shirt displaying a photograph of her husband. My mother was South African and my first book had been on apartheid. I wondered how an Afrikaans couple came to be running a hostel in Peckham. They were the only whites in the place.

They stared open-mouthed at Tuggy Tug. Then they stared at Swagger and me. 'We did not know you had friends like these,' said the wife. 'He's not allowed visitors,' said the husband. 'But for you, lady, we will make an exception.'

Tuggy Tug had not endeared himself to them. He smoked spliffs and had smuggled friends into his room after the 9 p.m. curfew.

Out on the street, Tuggy Tug suddenly faltered. He looked around fearfully and flapped his hands about his face. 'I miss my hood,' he said.

In the car he started speaking about his sister. He rarely mentioned his family. He never spoke about his parents – all of whose five children had been taken into care. His three older brothers were in and out of prison.

His sister was the youngest and studying for her GCSEs. None of the boys had come near to doing a GCSE. 'She sits and reads and no one make her. She does it all on her own,' he said in wonder. He went on in a rush, 'I love my sister. I really love that little girl.' As usual he saw love in terms of financial generosity. He went on, 'She ask me for anything and I give it to her, a bare twenty-pound note I give it so she can go to the cinema and do things with her friends. Because I never had no one give me nothing so I couldn't be a normal child when I was growing up. Nobody ever helped me with shit bruv. I am so on my own. You get me?' The removal of his hood had done more than transform his looks. It had opened him up and revealed how, in his mind, love and money were interchangeable.

He stared out of the window then shook his head. 'That's the hard life. So lonely waking up with no money in my pocket. I think no one knows what that feels like. No credit card. No job. No jobs centre. What you gonna do? What you gonna do? You can either live like a tramp or live normal. How do I live normal? How can I live normal?' His voice turned desperate. 'You have to rob. That's the God's honest truth like. That's no lie. You have to rob for your money bruv. Do something bruv, can't sit down.' He sighed then went on, 'Certain crimes you can't even do without money. That how real it is. You have to have money to do certain crimes.'

Tuggy Tug leaned forward to explain. 'You think you can sell drugs for free unless you got someone close to you? Well apart from that, that's not gonna work without money.' Drug dealers needed money to buy supplies. He nodded his head. 'If you ain't got money there's only one crime you can do poundless with zero money in your pocket and that's robberies. Cos you don't need a CV, you don't need to be black, you don't need to be white, you don't need to be shit, you just got to put your heart into it and rob. And that's the easiest thing. That's the God's honest easiest thing to do. And there's nothing else to do. If you can name one thing how to get me a little job, name me one God's honest thing left to do.'

Did he see a way out?

Tuggy Tug's mouth drooped with sadness. 'No. Don't see a way out of nothing. Nothing, there's no way out here I've realised that.'

Half an hour across the river and we entered another world. The Victorian dining room of the Liberal Club was all dark wood, glazed tiles and columns. Around us waiters served businessmen and civil servants from silver salvers. Against this backdrop I now found myself having lunch with three generations of robbers, two former and one potential. Over us loomed a life-sized marble statue of Gladstone.

Bobby Cummines was ordering. A small, dynamic man in his sixties, he had immediately felt a kinship with the equally small and dynamic Tuggy Tug. They might be a different colour, from different generations and different parts of London but here, declared Bobby, was his younger self. Tuggy Tug beamed. The promotion of the TV programme was pushed aside. Bobby had changed the agenda. This former hit man and armed robber had decided there were more important things to do. He had decided to save Tuggy Tug.

'Me and you,' said Bobby to Tuggy Tug, 'we were doing the same stuff. We grew up on the same street.' At sixteen, Bobby was jailed for possession of a sawn-off shotgun. He spent thirteen of the next twenty years in prison for offences including manslaughter and bank robbery. 'But the hardest thing I ever done was stacking shelves in Tesco when I decided to go straight.

'People ask do you regret the crime? And I say not at all. I was earning more money than the Prime Minister. Tugs believe me it is kicks, chicks and champagne. But he who eats the meal picks up the bill.' The waiter handed us the menu. I glanced over but Tuggy Tug was reading his with aplomb.

Bobby described life in prison. 'You are living in a toilet, eating next to a toilet with a cell mate who may not wash and has been banged up for so many fucking years he is like an animal or so sexually confused he starts sending you love letters.' He detailed the different ways you die in prison: the petrol bombs, scalding sugared water or just a biro stabbed into the throat. Swagger looked up from his menu. 'Yeah I had to do that one time,' he murmured. A big Rastafarian had come at him.

Bobby explained that in prison, 'Everyone is tooled up. It's not because you was nasty, it was because the "P" for "prison" stood for "paranoia". My friend had an argument with a guy cos they were cooking on a Sunday. The guy stabbed him to death over an onion. It was a butcher's boning knife stabbed through the heart. Dead instantly over an onion. That's how cheap life is in jail.'

The maître d'hôtel hovered behind Bobby, ready to take the order. Bobby ignored him. 'You don't do a prison sentence. You survive it.' Swagger nodded.

Tuggy Tug, confident after our meals together, now addressed the head waiter and demanded a steak, well done. I could see that the waiter barely understood him.

After the orders were taken Bobby returned to Tuggy Tug. 'We can talk about me later. Now tell me about you, Tugs.' Like an anxious mother at a school parents' meeting, I sought to explain, 'He's got no one looking after him.'

'Why is no one looking after you?' asked Bobby.

Embarrassed, Tuggy Tug shrugged. 'I don't really know. I just do me, man. It's hard to explain.'

Bobby leant back. 'I am sitting here, looking at you and what do I see? A smart intelligent young man, not a moron.' I clucked with approval. Tuggy Tug grinned. Bobby went on, 'You look sharp. You are a good-looking guy. I could dress you in any-thing and you look good. You got the build for it same as me. You are one of life's lucky people. You could put a sack of rags on us and we would still look good.' Bobby glanced down at his double-breasted suit, flicked the spotless lapel then returned to Tuggy Tug. 'So I want to know more about you. I don't want you banged up like a fucking animal for thirteen years because you are worth more than that.'

'Unfortunately he's on the road,' remarked Swagger.

'So what are you doing?' asked Bobby. 'I don't want you to grass yourself up but I want to know where you are coming from brother.'

Tuggy Tug said, 'I am not one of those guys who will do one thing. I will do everything. If you ain't got no money you can't do nothing, you get me. You got to try something every day and so that's what I do.'

Bobby eyed him meditatively. 'Anything that's going. We are all here to survive and where you are now is exactly where I was.'

Swagger interrupted to address Bobby: 'You need to be honest with him.'

As if guessing what was to follow, Tuggy Tug said, 'It's hard out there, trust me.'

Bobby nodded in agreement. 'When I was doing it on the street people got blinded, people got stabbed. I'm not making out I was a victim. I was doing people and I had no qualms about doing them. Because there was only one place I wanted to be and that was the top. There was no question of coming second.'

Tuggy Tug nodded. This he clearly agreed with. Bobby went on, 'To be that top man on the rock I had to be more vicious than anyone else on that rock. You know what I am saying? The only way you are going to be the governor is to be in control and the only way you get control is by fear, right?' Tuggy Tug had ceased his normal rapid glances and attention jumping. He became calm and focused on the older man.

I too was staring. I had not expected this. Here was one of life's hard men taking trouble with this lost boy. He was the first person Tuggy Tug had come across who wanted to help him – and in a way that was hitting home.

Bobby went on, 'When people say to me about respect I say to them don't talk crap. Respect is different. What we had was fear. People feared us. They didn't respect us, they feared us. That would do because they did not mess with us. Right, and that's exactly where you are now. I am talking right?'

The first course arrived. Tuggy Tug glanced sideways to check which fork Bobby picked up.

Bobby continued, 'Now I am going to take you on the journey where you are going to end up right and then you can't say at the end of this, Bobby no one fucking told me about this.'

Tuggy Tug said, 'The drugs pay right now. Like you just sit in your home and the money rolls in.'

Bobby just shook his head and repeated that Tuggy Tug was on a dangerous path. He described a situation. Imagine, he said, he was a supplier and he had three dealers. He allowed his suppliers to buy drugs on one week's credit. He lent number 1 three grand, number 2 two grand and number 3 one grand. 'I come and knock on your door. "Number 3, do you want this parcel?"'

'Yeah,' said Tuggy Tug.

Bobby nodded. 'You are number 3 and it's your parcel now and you are selling it.'

'Now come Friday, I am coming around for my dough. But no one can pay me back. So what do I do? I don't allow people to owe me money. There are only two ways I deal with you in this business. It's either with a pound coin or it's with a bullet in the head, OK? So I say to Swagger, we are working together, "I got to send a message out. We are owed too much money, all right. I am going to shoot one." So who am I going to whack?'

'Number one,' said Tuggy Tug instantly.

'No,' said Bobby, 'I shoot the young man who owes me the

least. I shoot number three. I shoot you.' Tuggy Tug stared open-mouthed, as the logic of this hit him. Bobby, it appeared, had judged to a T where in the drug chain Tuggy Tug stood.

Bobby was continuing, 'And when I come and get you, I know you carry a tool so I am all smiles' – he jumped to his feet and stepped up to Tuggy Tug, smiling. He walked past, whipped around, raised his fingers in the shape of a barrel and shot Tuggy Tug in the back of the head. We all froze. 'No fucking way you are coming back from that one,' said Bobby. He adjusted his cuffs, sat down and picked up his fork. After a moment he addressed Tuggy Tug: 'I know you, and you know why? Because I am looking at me, and you are on a very, very dangerous path my friend.'

The second course arrived. Tuggy Tug examined his steak and announced he could see the blood. Bobby called the waiter, over-ruled his excuses and sent it back. He then inspected his mush-rooms with the tip of his knife before ordering tomato ketchup. Tuggy Tug's eyes never left his face.

'Why do you think it's so hard to change?' Bobby asked him. 'How much jail time have you done Tugs?'

'I just got remanded.'

Swagger broke in. 'He hasn't been given the whack yet. He's yet to experience it.' Swagger went on, 'I tell you what is going through his mind. He's frightened of making that change. He prefers to sit down around his table with a big box of weed and draws and another big box beside him bagging out, his phone ringing, six or seven people moving it for him now. How is he going to let that go?'

I pointed out that I hoped to find a sales job for him. I thought Tuggy Tug would make a good salesman; Bobby was dismissive. That might pay at the most £14,000 a year, 'He can earn four hundred pounds in a morning.' A successful salesman could earn a lot more than that, I persisted.

Bobby sought to translate this into something with meaning for Tuggy Tug.

'When you get your gear, you test it to make sure it's good gear. You make sure it ain't Brixton mix don't you?' Tuggy Tug nodded. 'That's called quality control. When you are selling it you look around the area to see who is giving you the best price. Yeah? That's called market research, OK? When you getting rid of it, you are looking at who you are going to lay it on that's safe. You are using your networking.'

'Yeah,' agreed Tuggy Tug.

'The only thing you are doing in your life you are selling the wrong fucking product. Now if you were selling Chanel you are driving a Porsche. The copper comes knocking on your door and he's calling you Sir.'

A waitress now arrived with the pudding menus and coffee.

'I know what you are talking about,' conceded Bobby. 'It's the buzz. You don't want to lose that. That buzz is better than anything. Second is that camaraderie with your pals that you don't want to lose, that is a big lock-in. You lose a family, you gain a new family on the streets, your crew.'

'Yeah,' said Tuggy Tug softly.

'You know what I am saying? They are your family.'

I said I was trying to move them all up. Bobby shook his head at my naivety. 'He knows he can't get them involved because he would be seen as a wrong 'un and they would do him.' Bobby stirred his coffee. 'It's the hardest thing in that world, giving it up.'

'True, true,' said Swagger, who knew all too well how hard it was.

Bobby shook his head. 'I got nothing to gain from this, right? I couldn't give a shit if you walk out of here and say silly old bastard. But I know you. You know why, because I am looking at me and I am a nasty bastard in that world and you are going to grow up an even more nasty bastard in your world.

'So what's waiting for you? I can tell you. Most of my pals have been shot dead through gang war. The others are all doing thirty years or are sitting in a wheelchair where someone cut the back of their neck – the Yardies are notorious for that – cut the spinal cord and you are dead from the waist down and your mum is feeding you. That's the reality when you come up to this level, all right? The level you want to get to.

'Please never go there. I will tell you what it's like to be at the top table. We call it the top table. You got the chicks, the E-Type Jag. You got the Ferrari. You got it all. But it's for the moment. It's Tinseltown. It's an illusion. You are sitting there, you are the most popular guy in the world but you are on your own. You are in a crowd and you are on your own. Because you don't know who is going to grass you. You don't know who is going to pop you and you don't know if there is an undercover Old Bill lurking.'

Swagger remarked that the Old Bill were watching a friend of his, a successful drug dealer, 'and he's bought this nice flashy car and he's goin' to have to sell it now otherwise it going to send him to prison'.

Bobby considered Tuggy Tug as he tucked into a slice of chocolate cake. 'If I was still at it sure I would employ you.' Tuggy Tug looked up with alacrity. Bobby went on, 'You work for me and you do it right. I am going to guarantee you £100,000. I am going to give you £50,000 in cash up front.' Tuggy Tug had forgotten about the chocolate cake.

'What are you going to do for me? Are you going to be loyal to me?'

'Yeah,' breathed Tuggy Tug as if hypnotised.

'Totally loyal?'

'Yeah.'

'If I tell you I want you to carry my heroin from A to B for me are you going to do it?'

'Yeah.'

'I am going to give you that every year that you are with me and buy you the suit, the BMW. But if you fuck up you are on your own. If you go to jail you don't grass me and you don't talk. Have we got a deal?'

Tuggy Tug nodded hard.

'Would you pop someone for me? If I sent you out to shoot Swagger – not kill him, shoot him in the leg – would you pop Swagger?'

Tuggy Tug's eyes never left Bobby's face. 'Yeah,' he said.

Across the table Swagger and I looked at each other.

Bobby went on, 'But then you come to me. You got caught on camera. You are not an asset any more you are a liability. It doesn't matter if I like you or dislike you. You are now a bit of work. You are going to jail for ten years.' Tuggy Tug's mouth scrunched up in puzzlement. He could not see where this was going.

Bobby went on, 'But I look after you while you are in prison because I want to use you again when you come out. I am a nice guy. I send you in a bit of weed every week, some trainers. "Bobby's a good guy," you say, "Bobby looks after the family." What is it costing me? Peanuts. I got the junkies out there nicking for me so I am not even paying the real price of the trainers. What does it mean for me? Every day you are in jail, I am earning more money. I am out there and I have got the chicks and you are looking at magazines thinking about the women you could have. I have now placed you in the worst place with every nutter that is going to carve you up. Why? Because basically I have paid you to do my jail time. It's a good deal for me. But what about you?'

He pulled out a Montblanc fountain pen. 'How good does that £50,000 look now? It sounded such a big sum. You are in prison for ten years, that's £5,000 a year. How much does that work out a week?' He scribbled some figures and handed them to Tuggy Tug. 'You might as well have been on benefits. You could have made more on benefits,' said Bobby. Tuggy Tug did not move. He just held that bit of paper and stared at it.

Pleased at a job well done, Bobby leant back in his chair and looked around expansively. 'How do you like this club?' he asked Tuggy Tug.

Tuggy Tug said, 'I could hang here all day.'

Bobby said, 'I want to go on doing deals until I die so I like to know the new young men coming up. I will want to do deals with you.' Tuggy Tug just beamed.

All three men now went to the loo together. Later Swagger told me Tuggy Tug had announced, 'I just love this man,' and that he wanted to go home with him and never do crime again. 'It's deep,' remarked Swagger. As we walked out of the restaurant Tuggy Tug caught me. 'He said I must respect you,' he remarked with all the enthusiasm of a recent convert. He then hailed a waiter, addressed him as 'bruv' and told him he was going 'legit' now and would be returning in a few years as a member.

The three of us drove back euphoric. In a narrow street of Victorian houses off Tulse Hill, Tuggy Tug suddenly remarked that his grandmother lived here. Something in his voice made me ask, 'Would she like to see you in this suit?' We rang the doorbell but she did not answer. Swagger was all for leaving. I glanced at Tuggy Tug's face. 'Let's keep trying,' I said and began to rap hard on the glass.

Eventually a black woman in her seventies opened the door. She was wearing a hat and coat and stared with astonishment at Tuggy Tug. She led us into the front sitting room stuffed with a grand piano, bookshelves, photographs on every surface and a huge fish tank.

Daphne was in fact his foster mother and had cared for him for six years from the age of five to eleven. 'All the good in me', said Tuggy Tug by way of an introduction, 'is because of the time I spent with her.' For the last few years, he had avoided Daphne. He was ashamed and did not want her to see him disintegrate. 'He was such a loving child,' she said.

He had no recollection of his early years. 'My mind is a blank on anything before I got here. I don't even remember arriving here.' He had blotted out all memory of his crack addict mother. 'My first memory is of her,' he said of Daphne.

When she reached retirement age, the council insisted she give up Tuggy Tug and his sister. Tuggy Tug said, 'They did not take us easy. We put up a fight.' I imagined social workers dragging the two screaming children from the only mother they had known. It was just one example of the routine cruelty I had heard about so often while researching a think-tank report on our care system. 'That's when it all went wrong,' said Tuggy Tug. Not surprisingly his behaviour deteriorated. He went from one foster family to the next, finally ending up in a children's home for troubled youngsters.

I told Daphne she should be proud of Tuggy Tug. He had behaved perfectly and had impressed a big man. He had what it takes to succeed.

She could not get over the sight of him in a suit. She exclaimed and clapped her hands and made much of him. He stood there, straight-backed, hands folded in front of him and a look of such pride and accomplishment on his face that it made me want to cry. He said, 'I will help you do the gardening, Nana, do you want something dug?' She glanced outside at the frozen ground.

When we returned to his room, he took off the suit and put his hoodie back on. I showed him how to floss his teeth. For the first time I touched him, stroked his cheek and kissed him. He said, 'A hundred per cent in my heart I want to get working, that's the bottom line.'

He left with us, even shaking the hand of his old enemy, the white South African at the front door. He was all soft, peaceful and aglow as he walked up the street. Swagger climbed into the car with me and said, 'He's off to tell his friends. They won't understand.' He retrieved a cigarette from behind his ear and lit it. 'If he is to get on and succeed, he'll have to break with them. But they are all he has. They are his family. He won't cope with the loneliness it will take to break with them. I know,' he added, 'I am so lonely myself.'

That evening I received a drop call from Mash. I phoned him back and he invited me to a football match. He was playing for a club outside London. The manager's attitude was clear: £100 if they won a match and £20 if they lost. I was delighted. Swagger had asked around and been told that Mash was really gifted at football.

I told Mash that I had heard he had been involved in stealing the copper tiles from the roof of the former community centre. Mash was indignant. He had let Tuggy Tug and his gang go. In revenge they were putting around lies about him. He was very convincing and I did not know who to believe. He returned to his football career. There was one problem. The club wanted him there three times a week for training but he did not have the train fare. He was having to skank a ride (travel without paying) and was afraid of getting arrested again and losing everything. If he turned up for six months, they would take him on. This meant a salary and somewhere to live. I said I would talk to the manager and maybe pay the fare myself. I felt a glow of accomplishment. Here were Mash and Tuggy Tug about to become success stories. If I could show they could do it, then why not the many other young men in our inner cities whose lives are being needlessly wasted?

Seventeen

Now that Tuggy Tug wanted a job, it was time to impress on him what he must be prepared to do and how hard he would have to work. On a blowy day in early spring I met Tuggy Tug and Lips in Swagger's flat.

We had planned to go out but the night before Swagger's girl-friend had turned up with their son, Tshane. She had thrown Swagger out after he lost his previous job. Now she was all stressed, she said, and could not cope. She was leaving the little boy with Swagger and maybe coming back in two weeks. 'I says to her I says, "Stop getting your dollies out of the pram, I'll take the little man."' I thought he had been banned from going near her. What about the court case? And the job interviews he had lined up? He would have to cancel those now. 'It's madness,' agreed Swagger.

So instead we picnicked in his flat on carrot cake, buns stuffed with a spicy green vegetable and salt mackerel with green banana and dumplings cooked by Swagger's mother.

Swagger's sitting room looked out over a children's play-ground. The sun poured in. A painting of a palm tree blown by the wind hung over a flat-screen TV. Bags with designer labels dangled from the door handle. On the windowsill an empty bottle of Moët & Chandon propped up a life-size photograph of Tshane.

Tuggy Tug, Lips and I squashed up on the only piece of fur-niture – a green leather Chesterfield sofa. Swagger was perched on an empty pot of Dulux paint. As usual, Lips had not removed his anorak or hat and was sitting hunched up and almost hidden. Tuggy Tug was leaning forward to roll a joint and joking with Swagger, who suddenly leapt up to shout at the pigeons. He did not like them landing on his balcony. 'I told the council, put a net up there or else I'll be shootin' them next,' he said.

Tshane was asleep and we were making the most of it.

Tuggy Tug waved his carton of Ribena at me for emphasis as we discussed pay. He assured me, 'It don't have to be big money but something that you can save and survive off the same time.' I was surprised at this talk of saving. Tuggy Tug had never struck me as a saver. It turned out I was wrong. He had it all worked out. He went on, 'If you were getting a job that paid you two bills a week, then you can survive off a bill a week and save a bill a week. That's the perfect job. Everyone would be nicer for that and bills getting stacked every week and you can spunk a bill a week.' He sighed. 'You'd be nice. That's called a perfect job: two bills a week. No reason why not give a man that bruv. You get me?'

I could not argue. It seemed a lot cheaper than keeping Tuggy Tug in prison for roughly four times that amount a week.

Tuggy Tug had given this business of 'going legit' a lot of thought. He had identified one problem. 'You get a job that pays two bills a week,' he said, but then that is the sort of job 'where they take tax out of your money'. He knew how much too, 'It's eighty pounds so you get left with one twenty a week.' Tuggy Tug saw no incentive to work after paying tax. How could he save when 'You got to buy, you know, travel money to get to work, something to eat during the week. So how much money are you really saving? Like forty pounds a week. That's forty pounds a week done. Finito. Some waste man something!'

'See,' said Swagger.

Tshane began to stir. Swagger went into the bedroom and we heard him crooning to the waking child as he changed its nappy. 'Here's my little man,' he said, standing at the door with Tshane in his arms. He had Swagger's wide head, clown eyes and mobile features but his little face was alive and fresh and gazed at us with trusting eyes. Swagger set him on the sofa where the child blinked, looked around then opened his mouth to wail. Swagger shushed him. He bent down to clean Tshane's eyes, fussing with a tissue, then blew him kisses. The little boy gazed affronted at Swagger, then with great concentration smacked his lips back at his father. Swagger laughed. 'We all good here?' He broke off a piece of carrot cake and popped it into the child's mouth.

Tuggy Tug glanced at Tshane as one would a wild and unpredictable animal then resumed his conversation. I had asked him how much was the minimum he would take for a week's work.

He replied, 'Two bills with no tax. That way I'm spending a hundred pounds and you get a hundred pounds a week.' He paused to twiddle his straw in the juice box. 'A hundred pounds a week is nothing for a man my age, yeah, but obviously having a job and trying to come from nowhere is a start, you feel me? So a man will spend the one bill a week and save one bill knowing that it's not getting taxed. You know it's there, innit? You get money in your pocket to spend and save it.'

'So you saying you want two hundred pounds in your pocket every week?' said Swagger. 'You are not the only one who would like that bruv.'

'Yeah every week and I'll do that legit,' promised Tuggy Tug.

What did he think of starting on £150 a week? Maybe I could get him something for that. Tshane launched himself off the sofa, grabbed the glass table beneath the TV, staggered then flexed his legs a few times and looked triumphantly at us.

Tuggy Tug swivelled his legs away from the child. 'That's

something, you get me,' he said of my offer. 'You can always work for a rise and that. Everything's possible for that, you get me? So that's nothing, starting from nowhere one fifty away from the two hundred I want? That's nothing. Twenty-five pounds in the bank less a week that's it. Survive off seventy-five pounds and save seventy-five pounds. Feel me?'

Swagger lurched forward to catch Tshane. 'It just drops in your bank fam,' he agreed. He began to roll a spliff while holding Tshane between his knees. He went on, 'There's still gonna have to be a lot of input into you fam, to keep making sure you go to work. Getting a job maybe we're halfway there.' He licked the Rizla. 'Or maybe even quarter of the way. There's going to be like behavioural problems. You not used to being disciplined by somebody. Young men that are on the road like you coz and not working for a long time, you find that you become your own bosses. You become independent in your own way. Nobody's telling you what to do and what not to do. So the minute you go into a work setting and somebody's telling you what to do, it can be hard to take on. It's going to be challenging for you.' He lit his spliff. Tshane seized his chance to wriggle free and set off on a drunken promenade of the room.

I said to Tuggy Tug that he was good at what he was doing. He was going to have to start again in a new world with new rules. And what about leaving the old life behind?

Lips suddenly spoke up. He turned to Tuggy Tug. 'See the way the hood's in your blood right now. So let me ask you a question: if you had ten bags now yeah, tell me that you're not gonna buy something that involves hood or that involves you coming to the hood to buy? Or would you spend it straight, ten bags of good stuff out there? Or would you not come to the hood and try to make some sort of wholesale money?' (He meant invest £1,000 buying drugs in order to turn a profit.)

Tuggy Tug considered this. He said, 'I'll dip in the hood and I'll dip there, I'd take good things from everywhere. Anything I see, I hand-pick shit and put it together blud.'

Lips roused himself to lean forward. 'I hear that but would you come to the hood to get something? Right would your lidge [legitimately earned] money be spent in the hood on something that it shouldn't be spent? See that's what I want to know fam.'

I said I wanted to know that too. There was no half and half here. If he started working, he could not combine that with crime. Both boys looked unconvinced.

Tuggy Tug reassured me, 'Obviously I wanna touch legit man and what comes from that blud and how easy it is to make that.' (He wants to make money legitimately and enjoy everything that comes from living within the law.) He paused, sighing. 'I know what I'm leaving behind if I don't fuck with the hood any more. See I got real hood man genes in me yeah. I'll always come to the hood.'

Lips, who had collapsed back into his anorak, nodded. 'Yeah cos obviously you can't blow up and leave everyone man.' Yet on the other hand, 'Going legit it feels clean bruv.'

I thought of the impossibility of getting my son to abandon his group of friends and his background. Yet this is what Tuggy Tug had to do – and for a life he could not yet envisage.

Tshane now reached the kitchen, where he pointed in the air and announced, 'Bee.' We all looked at him. He pointed again with growing impatience. 'Bee, bee.' Swagger got up, opened the fridge door and gave him a carton of juice. He sat down again. Tshane finished the juice, dropped the box, spent a few moments stamping on it then, satisfied it was dead, lurched back into the sitting room. On the way he spotted what lay on top of Swagger's speaker – a can of spray polish, air-freshener, a statue of the three wise monkeys and a Jamaican ratchet knife. He pointed at the knife. 'Bee,' he urged. Tuggy Tug's eyes fixed on the knife too.

Swagger got up hurriedly and retrieved the knife. 'I bought this from Jamaica. They're old-school. That's what you call a free-style ratchet. You can't buy them here.' Tuggy Tug was suddenly out of the sofa and snatching the knife from Swagger's hands. Tshane was hanging on to his father's legs, staring at the weapon. Tuggy Tug said, 'I'll give you a tenner for it.'

Swagger said, 'In Jamaica, people either carry one of those or an ice pick.' 'Or a gun,' said Lips, who had been at school in Jamaica.

Tuggy Tug was delighted with the knife. 'Have you seen me with this? Man needs this Swagger.' Tshane started towards Tuggy Tug and the knife.

Swagger said, 'You a joker man,' then glanced at his son. 'Those things shouldn't attract you neither!' He tried to take the knife from Tuggy Tug, who held on. 'I'll give it back to you before I go man. Blud your time soon expire, just give the man the knife blud.'

Swagger said, 'So I can hear next week that you've been arrested with a knife?'

Tuggy was indignant. 'No, I'm not rolling with it like that!'

Swagger snorted. 'What you gonna do? Leave it in your house?'

Tuggy Tug said, 'No, just when I'm going out there, on special occasions.' The tension dissipated. Swagger and I burst out laughing.

'There's no special occasions,' he said.

'Not at all,' I said.

'Not even for half an hour?' asked Tuggy Tug, blowing up his cheeks with disappointment. Swagger leant over him, speaking calmly and firmly as you would to a child. 'It came from Jamaica. It come in my suitcase as an ornament and it stays on my speaker box and doesn't leave my house.' He took the knife off Tuggy Tug and put it back. 'It doesn't leave,' he said. Tshane burst into tears.

Swagger went into the kitchen, found a wooden spoon and started playing it off all the surfaces. 'Look at this Tshane, look, look,' and he played the little boy away from the speaker and towards the window. There he picked him up and showed him the seagulls wheeling outside.

That over, we returned to our previous conversation. Would Tuggy Tug be able to abandon the hood? Tuggy Tug, ever practical, hedged his bets. 'I don't know because until something works out for me, I'm here innit. I can't just stop what I'm doing. If nothing works out for me, I'll be back. If something works then I can stop what I'm doing. Apart from that you have to keep trying every day if you wanna live this life. You got one life blud.'

Swagger looked around and shook his head. 'Your brain's trapped, bruv. You hear what I mean. Your mind's still in the hood.' Tshane squirmed free, tottered back towards the kitchen, seized the spoon and now hit the TV screen. Swagger got up, clapped his hands and lured the child away again.

He went on, 'But it's good you're at work. You're doing something good. And it's boring dealing drugs, I can tell you. You think it's all hustle and bustle now? You wait. Standing around on a street corner waiting for your phone to ring. You know I was talking to my friend who sells heroin. He is waking up in the morning hungry and he can't eat until a heroin addict calls him to get a little ting. What kind of life is that? And he's a big man, over thirty.'

But Tuggy had picked up his mobile and was not listening. 'Phone me when you get close,' he urged his friend. He asked Swagger to throw him his lighter and said, 'I think I'm gonna visit my mate in Maudsley [the psychiatric hospital in South

London].' This turned out not to be Bulldog as I had assumed but a boy I did not know. Swagger said, 'Is he in the Maudsley? For what? Smoking skunk?'

Tuggy Tug shrugged. 'He lied and said he smoked. He's smoked a few but it's cos he's dumb sudden in the head and he moves a bit slow like. He's on food [crack].' Swagger explained for my benefit, 'So they believed him and they're trying to get him help through the mental health system.'

Tuggy Tug leant forward. 'Someone said they visited him and he's just normal fam like and they don't understand why he's there.' Swagger wondered if it was better than prison. Tuggy Tug was dismissive: 'They just knock a man out. Me personally I believe there should be some sort of medical check to really see if he's mad or not. Cos they're gonna drug up a perfectly good person.'

Swagger agreed. 'And he could come out madder. He wasn't mad when he went in.'

Tuggy Tug got out his second phone, glanced at it then stood up to leave, 'A man's got schedules to do blud.'

I told him to behave. Tuggy Tug pointed at himself, straightened up, chin tilted to the ceiling, and declared, 'You're looking at a multimillionaire blud . . .'

Swagger snorted. 'A multimillionaire in the making yeah? You got to make a little change.'

The boys left. Tshane began to grizzle. 'He's not well,' said Swagger, cupping his son's head with the same lumps and bumps as his own and kissing him. Tshane seemed well enough to me. Swagger took him onto his lap and began to rock the little boy, humming a rap song to him. From under a cushion on the sofa, he pulled out some weed, a few unpaid bills and finally a copy of the children's book *The Very Hungry Caterpillar*. He began to read to Tshane, turning the pages and wriggling his fingers through the holes in them. Tshane stuck his thumb in his mouth and started to stroke his knee contentedly.

I got up to leave. Swagger said that this time we had to succeed with Tuggy Tug. 'We have to get him into a job or college or some form of training that's positive and get him away from all the madness that he's stuck in at the moment. If we don't then there's three outcomes. He'll go to prison, he'll end up dead, stabbed, or he'll end up in an institution, a mental health institution on account of the amount he's smoking. So it's a bad situation and why it's so bad as well is it's not just him, it's thousands of young men with the same prospects, and them little boys yet to grow up.'

He went on rocking Tshane.

Eighteen

A month later we entered a bitter spring. The need to find a job for Tuggy Tug now consumed me. Swagger's remarks had given a new urgency to saving him. I felt responsible for his conversion and I could not let him down. The encounter with his foster mother had revealed another side to the gang leader which had touched me deeply and offered hope of a different future. I was so wrapped up in Tuggy Tug, I did not give a thought to Swagger or what his involvement was costing him. I knew that Tuggy Tug had raised uncomfortable issues for Swagger over his past. I did not think of Swagger's future.

At a think-tank event I met an entrepreneur. Scott was in his thirties and starting businesses all over the world. He complained it was difficult to find good salesmen in the UK. 'We are an English company but we have no English staff. It is just too much trouble.' I had always thought Tuggy Tug would make an excellent salesman.

The year before Scott had interviewed fifty-two graduates. On paper they looked 'brilliant students'. Each had three As at A level and a 2:1 degree. He shook his head. 'There's a big difference between people passing exams and being ready for work.'

This was obvious even before the interviews began. Out of the fifty-two applicants, half arrived late. Only three of the fifty-two walked up to Scott, looked him in the eye, shook his hand and said good morning. The rest 'just ambled in'. When he asked them to solve a problem, only twelve had come equipped with a pad and pencil. The three who had greeted him proved the strongest candidates and he hired them. Within a year they were out due to their 'lackadaisical' attitude. They did not turn up on time in the morning. For the first six months, a manager had to check every one of their emails for spelling and grammar. They did not know how to learn. It was the first time they had ever been asked to learn on their own. Their ability 'to engage in business' was 'incredibly' disappointing and 'At five thirty on the dot, they left the office.'

I told Scott about Tuggy Tug. Tuggy Tug might not be able to use spell check but he could sell anything to anyone. Above all he was hungry, if not desperate, to succeed. If he thought there was a chance of making money, there would be no knocking off at 5.30 p.m. Scott was intrigued, but above all saw it as an opportunity to help and make a difference to someone's life. He told me to get Tuggy Tug to phone him. That was where the problems began.

A week later Scott complained that he had yet to hear from Tuggy Tug. I called the would-be reformed gang leader but could not get through to him. Instead I rang Smalls, who at that time always picked up my calls. 'Yo,' he said, 'are you all right then, Harry?' Unlike when my friends asked me the same question, this salutation from one of the boys always seemed to demand a proper response. I paused, seeking to translate my problems into something that would amuse and satisfy the concern of a seventeen-year-old heroin dealer. I told him my son had broken his nose for the third time playing rugby. Otherwise everything was fine. 'Shit happens,' remarked Smalls.

I then explained why I was calling. 'This little job then,' asked Smalls in his soft, high voice, 'how is it different from a job in Iceland?' I was taken aback. I thought Tuggy Tug had grasped the potential of the job. I understood now why he was ignoring my calls. I said it was the difference between a bike and a

Rolls-Royce. 'Yes I get that,' said Smalls, 'a Rolls and a bike that makes it clear.' He said he would pass this on to Tuggy Tug. He then added that he would be away for ten days. My heart sank. I dreaded to think where he was going. The last time was to sell heroin to undergraduates in a university town. I begged him to be careful.

As I put down the phone, I wondered at my concern. I never thought I would care what happened to a heroin dealer. But then I had never imagined a heroin dealer would be a serious, likeable young man the same age as my son.

Smalls obviously repeated our conversation because the next time I tried Tuggy Tug, he picked up. 'I been phoning, Harry, honest,' he said. But had he left a message? I persisted. There was a stunned silence. 'I never left a message in all my life,' said Tuggy Tug. It was true. The boys and Swagger always made drop calls to save on credit.

I wondered how to explain telephone etiquette south of the river to Scott – because there was an etiquette and a strong one. A drop call meant I had to phone back. The boys would see my name and pick up. However, they would be worried about answering a caller labelled Unknown. Unknown could be the police, the bailiffs or any number of people they did not want to talk to. It was why losing a phone was such a disaster. None of the gang would ever give out another member's number without confirmation from him. If I wanted to talk to someone on the periphery of the gang, I had to wait until he saw someone I knew and they remembered to ask his permission. Sometimes the process took months.

In the end I phoned Scott. I appreciated that getting Tuggy Tug to ring him was part of a test of his keenness but, what with Tuggy Tug's fluctuating credit and Scott's foreign travel, 'This could go on for the next year,' I said.

Tuggy Tug had been talking about the job because that afternoon Scott forwarded a text to me. It was from Belly, a cousin of Tuggy Tug's. The cousin explained he had heard Scott was offering jobs. He went on, 'I was interested and willing to work and learn fast whatever it would take to be a good employee. I guess you are a busy person and I would appreciate if you could get back to me if that offer still stands. I am twenty-four and serious about what was told to me from Tugs.' I said I had met the cousin. 'He is a decent young man,' I said. Then added as an afterthought, 'Of course he has been in jail for four years on a firearms offence.' There was a pause. Scott said, 'Harriet, do you think you might be spending too much time south of the river?'

Tuggy Tug meanwhile had offered Swagger an Apple Mac for £200. 'Our little rugrat is back on the road again. He is doing burglary now,' remarked Swagger gloomily. His girlfriend had removed Tshane as abruptly as she had left him and he was missing his child.

Scott suggested we meet up in his office after work one evening. I rang Tuggy Tug. 'I am on a tag, innit,' he said, 'I have to be back by five or I am in trouble.' I now had to explain to Scott that his prospective employee was on a curfew and persuade him to come to a hostel in Peckham. Scott appeared unfazed. He mentioned he was returning from New York on the red eye that morning and leaving for Paris in the evening. In between he was happy to visit Tuggy Tug.

I rang back Tuggy Tug. As usual he appeared to be wandering through streets made alien by their noise and commotion. Above the din, he shouted, 'I am in breach innit.'

It took me some time to understand that the tag was not the only problem. Since our last phone call, Tuggy Tug had breached the conditions of staying in the hostel. The South African couple had told him to leave. Once again he was homeless.

I rang his hostel and got the wife. Desperate now, I told her that my mother was from Cape Town. '*Sis boki!*' she replied. 'So are we!' She told me their surname. How extraordinary, I said, quite truthfully, my great-grandmother had the same surname. We contemplated this coincidence. 'We love it here,' she continued. 'We have been here for eight years.'

My Afrikaner credentials now established, I moved on to Tuggy Tug. I understood that he was a handful but could he stay just one more night? I explained the situation. It was such an opportunity for him. She sighed. 'We told him to take his things and go to the council,' she said. 'I will have to talk to my man.'

I phoned back Tuggy Tug. He said of his landlord, 'He's not listening, Harry you don't understand.' I heard him stop a passer-by and cadge a cigarette. An agonised howling suddenly erupted. 'What's that?' I demanded.

'Oh that's just a madman,' said Tuggy Tug, unconcerned. Could he find somewhere else to stay tonight? 'I ain't got no money to go down to housing,' he said.

I rang back the hostel. Reluctantly she agreed to let Tuggy Tug stay one more night. 'I am so fond of him,' she protested, 'when he smokes weed in his room, I am so disappointed; I can hardly sleep at night. My man doesn't like to see me so upset.'

I rang back Tuggy Tug, told him to tidy his room, open the windows and obey their rules for the next few hours at least.

Tuggy Tug was elated. 'I make it to the end of the month then I will be clear out of there and in a job,' he said triumphantly.

Finally I set off to Brixton to pick up Swagger. But he too had his problems. 'It's the bailiffs,' he said.

'Bailiffs?' I asked.

He did not want to leave his flat to come down to me. He thought the bailiffs might arrive at any moment. Why were the bailiffs after him? 'Same old same old,' said Swagger.

Even as he was trying to help the boys, Swagger had his own battles. After the abrupt end to his last charity job, Swagger had applied for agency work in catering. A job made his girlfriend happy. The company sent him to Twickenham for the rugby. He explained, 'It was all foreigners. I was the only English person working there, the only person speaking you know proper English, able to have a jaw with the customers.' He had first worked behind the bar. 'Yeah and I used the till and all,' he said. 'They trusted me with the money.'

He had enjoyed the job and been promoted to serve in the VIP area. 'My communication skills,' he said proudly. He asked management if he could work full-time. They agreed to take him on but only if he stopped working for the agency first. There had to be a three-month grace period before they could employ him. Swagger stopped and that was when things started to go wrong.

'If I am honest,' he said, 'tings had been going pear-shape before that.' He soon discovered why no other English people were doing the job. On incapacity benefit Swagger received £140 every two weeks as well as the rent for his flat. This was another surprise. He did not look incapacitated to me. 'It's my depression,' announced Swagger. 'Not seeing my son does my head in.' He said no one liked going to the job centre to collect benefits because the people there 'are horrible'. Swagger was paid incapacity benefit directly into his bank account – its great virtue. He said everyone he knew either claimed for depression or a bad back because they were the easiest to fake.

The agency charged Twickenham over £300 for every worker they supplied; Swagger received £150. The first pay packet had been a shock. He had earned just £110; £40 had gone on tax. 'But why are you paying tax?' I asked, dumbfounded. 'This is the first money you have made this year.'

'It's the system, innit Harry,' he said, equally nonplussed. Swagger was paying something called emergency tax which kicks in when a person first starts a job after a long absence. 'I have to pay it for six months until they work out my band,' said Swagger miserably. It hardly seemed a good way to encourage people into a job. But there was worse. Now that Swagger was working, he had to pay rent of £70 a week out of that £110. So after getting up at 5 a.m., not to mention the expense of transport and a uniform, Swagger made £40 a week – £30 less than when he was on incapacity benefit. I said I certainly would not get a job if it cut my income by almost half. 'See,' said Swagger, 'now you understand why no one works around here.'

When he stopped working, he found himself with another problem. Housing benefit took time to start up again. He now owed the council rent. The council had called the bailiffs. Swagger managed to scrape together the money to pay the debt but, explained the council, it was too late. Once summoned, bailiffs, like some municipal genie, could not be called off. I offered to phone them and sort it out. If I could deal with the hostel, I could deal with bailiffs. 'I will have to go to court,' said Swagger. 'And I was hoping to keep away from them places.'

I phoned the bailiffs. After a long wait a man with an Essex accent admitted that he managed the account. I said I was ready to pay the £177. But I was not the only one taking note of accents. After hearing mine, the man announced, 'It's gone up to £388.40, sweetheart.'

'That's nearly double,' I exclaimed.

'We've had expenses since yesterday,' he said. 'Take it or leave it.'

'I want to talk to the manager,' I said.

'You must be joking,' he said and hung up.

I sat in my car overwhelmed. It was a new sensation. For the first time there was nothing I could do and no authority to appeal to. I got an inkling of what Swagger and Tuggy Tug felt every day of their lives. Movies like to portray street life as carefree and ebullient. You might have nothing but you click your fingers to imaginary beats and enjoy freedom. That was not my experience. Tuggy Tug and Swagger spent their time and energy on dealing with very small sums of money or very large bureaucracies. I felt drained and depressed. There seemed no way out – apart from crime.

Suddenly someone rapped on the side window. Swagger in a black coat, his clown face enfolded in its sweeping, upturned collar, grinned at me. He had climbed out of the window and down four floors. 'My burglary days,' he said by way of explanation. He looked around then jumped into the car. 'Put the pedal to the metal, Princess, and let's get out of here.'

Tuggy Tug's room was indeed tidy but smelt of spunk and expensive aftershave. I moved to the window, which I found propped open with a speaker. I tried to open it further. The speaker fell to the floor and the window banged closed. Tuggy Tug looked at me. 'The window's mash up, Harry,' he said patiently. 'That's why the speaker is there, innit.' He put the speaker back and reset the window.

I sat on the only chair. Tuggy Tug now began to describe how he and his friend had attacked a crack dealer. His friend had hit the crack dealer on the head. Here Tuggy Tug picked up an exploded balloon from the floor to illustrate the effect this had on the dealer. 'Bang and he just all wobbled away,' he exclaimed.

I said this was hardly the thing to be talking about before a job interview. I leant forward to make my point. The chair broke and I hit the ground. Swagger immediately reached out both hands and pulled me up. Tuggy Tug just looked on. When I remonstrated, he said, 'Well I was in shock, innit?'

I went outside to wait in the cold for Scott, who was lost. It was at this critical point that Swagger decided to run up the street for a chicken takeaway and cigarettes. 'I ain't eaten all day. How could I get out with the bailiffs and all?' he said. In his absence, Scott arrived and I took him up. The manager watched from the bottom of the stairs.

Tuggy Tug was standing at his bedroom door, fiddling with the lock – the third thing I had broken in that small, sparse room within ten minutes. He shot a glance at Scott then concentrated on the lock, saying to me, 'You ain't twisted it right when you left. You got to twist it right. It's not one of them doors that just closes.'

I pulled him away from the lock and introduced him to Scott. Tuggy Tug stared, speechless. Scott, like any successful business-man, wore a well-cut suit and an expensive watch – Tuggy Tug and Swagger, as they later told me, spotted the make instantly – but in a Peckham hostel he might as well have been a god visiting from another world. Tuggy Tug shrunk in front of my eyes, his personality dimmed by Scott's alien splendour.

Swagger now returned and the room filled with the smell of fried chicken.

Scott sat on the bed next to Tuggy Tug and asked to see his tag then questioned him about his crimes. Tuggy Tug pulled up a leg of his tracksuit bottoms, barely coherent.

Swagger and I decided to leave them to it. We went outside and walked around the block in the dark and the cold like anxious parents. Was there any hope for our boy? Would he recover and shine?

When we returned, they were still sitting on the bed. Tuggy Tug had slouched against the wall, his mouth so swollen with disappointment that it had lost all trace of indentation. I had badly miscalculated. I had built up his expectations with the promise of a salesman job that he had not a hope of getting. The confidence in which I had placed such store did not transfer past a few streets or the life he knew.

Scott said he could not help Tuggy Tug until he got some education. 'Why should I do it all for you?' he said.

'Listen to what the big man tells you,' said Swagger.

But we had lost Tuggy Tug and undone all Bobby Cummines's good work. He got more and more resistant. He ignored Scott, refused to meet my eye and addressed himself to Swagger as one criminal to another.

I walked Scott to his car, which was miraculously untouched. Scott professed himself shocked. Tuggy Tug was so far removed from anything he could relate to or understand. 'He can't even speak properly. He couldn't even get a job sweeping the floor of a Kentucky Fried Chicken!' he said in wonder. Meeting him had opened his eyes. He said, 'I had no idea such people existed.' The gap between Tuggy Tug and a boy from his own background left him aghast. 'It's like another country,' he repeated twice. He wanted to help but was unsure how.

When I returned to the house, the manager opened the door. Despite the cold, he wore only a vest and underpants and had a mournful look.

Back upstairs Tuggy Tug admitted he had found it difficult to talk to Scott. 'But you talk to me!' I said. He gave me the engaging smile I had so wanted Scott to see. 'Yeah but I am like comfortable with you, Harry.'

I had failed with Tuggy Tug, but I also found myself failing with Mash too. I had been ringing Mash's football manager, who was enthusiastic about his ability. If Mash continued to turn up for practice, in a few months the club would take him on, give him a salary and a flat to share with other trainees. Until then I planned to buy Mash a railcard and provide some spending money to help him out. But over the last year, I had lost some of my gullibility. Something about the manager made me pause. I rang the club and asked for him. They had no one of that name working there as a coach. Swagger reported that Mash had got a friend to pose as his manager. 'I been telling you,' reproved Swagger. 'He's got his father and his uncles. He wants to be a big man like them. It's a waste. They say he's bad on the ball [talented at football].'

I rang Mash but he never picked up. Finally I tried his home line. He had been the only boy to provide me with a landline. His mother answered. She was indignant. 'He gave you this hard-luck story. It's all lies,' she said. 'He's had the best of everything. You should see his room. Do you know how much I paid for a roll of his wallpaper? He's got the latest equipment, everything the best. He lies to you. He lies to me. He's a horrible person. You come and see for yourself. He's horrible, horrible, horrible . . .' Her voice was rising into near-madness. I put down the phone. I could not listen any more. I had started to shake.

Nineteen

The weather finally improved. On a warm, wet day in early summer, I was driving Swagger, Smalls, Lips and Tuggy Tug to the job centre. I had failed to get Tuggy Tug a job in the private sector. Now we would try the state. In the back Tuggy Tug was wiping his face and complaining. It had taken a bribe of £30 before he would set foot in the place.

I was more optimistic. Here were people trained and paid to deal with a typical NEET – a young person not in education, employment or training. The government website had promised help into work. They seemed to understand that the cost of keeping Tuggy Tug in the criminal justice system was a lot more than training him for a job.

At first glance, the job centre exuded conviviality and purpose. Posters on the wall enquired if we were being treated correctly. Then the burly men in suits clustered around the door moved forward and announced we had to register. I smiled and said we was just looking thank you and swept everyone past them.

Smalls and Tuggy Tug showed me the computer displaying jobs. We went through one by one. Waiting and bar jobs looked hopeful but they were all temporary. 'They tell you to take it,' Smalls explained. 'So you sign off. Then the job ends and it's three weeks before your benefits begin again.' In the mean time, 'You are left with no money and bills to pay.'

Even jobs that looked promising required training and qualities out of reach of my boys. A job in retail, for example, stated the 'successful candidate must be numerate, reliable and enjoy working as part of a team'. My heart sank: except for the last, that ruled out everyone including Swagger – and it was temporary. Carpet cleaning looked hopeful but that needed 'experience with carpets and upholstery and a full, clean driving licence'.

Tuggy Tug snorted. 'They all say you need training. I don't know but there's even a special kind of training you need to stack shelves in Iceland, trust me fam.'

I turned to one of the burly men. Where did we go for advice? 'Upstairs,' he grunted. I glanced around. New green screens partitioned about a dozen desks at which job centre staff sat doing nothing. Otherwise the place was empty. Why could I not speak to an adviser here?

'That's for single mothers,' said the burly man.

I asked for the lift. The man looked at my retinue. Lips and Tuggy Tug were play-punching one another. Smalls loomed over us, unsmiling. The place had even affected Swagger, who had lowered his head as if for a fight. 'You can't use the lift,' he stated.

Swagger, sensing my irritation, took advantage. 'I've got a bad knee,' he complained, jettisoning the fighting stance for one of pain and pleading, 'and her hip ain't too good neither.' I left him arguing with the man while the boys and I took the stairs. At the top Swagger emerged triumphant from the lift. 'I am here every week claiming benefits,' he said. (Since he had lost his incapacity benefit when he'd started working, he was now collecting Jobseeker's Allowance.) 'You can't let them get you down.'

A light-skinned black woman called Anita took charge of us. I explained I was Tuggy Tug's mentor and we were here to find him a job. Her mouth, round and full, fractionally twitched. She got on the phone but had great difficulty finding the right person. 'I will get there eventually,' she said.

Which category did an eighteen-year-old on income support

come under? she asked. This required a lot of discussion. I was astonished. Surely they were dealing with young men from that category all the time. Why did it require so many transfers to different departments? And why did the discussion centre on benefits – rather than training or a job?

She made a point of explaining to each of her colleagues that the young man had a *mentor* with him.

I fetched Tuggy Tug, who was fooling around on the stairs with Lips. He slouched in, assuming the same shut-down expression as Mash had worn in Connexions. Reluctantly he sat in front of her, pushing himself down into the seat, his trousers slung so low, the crotch almost reached his knees. He pulled his wool Nike hat down over his forehead as if, with a bit of luck, he could creep inside and hide.

She asked for his national insurance number and he reeled it off. Noticing my surprise, he said, 'You got to remember that when you come to these places.'

Swagger added, 'Prison numbers and your national insurance number – you never forget those.'

I pointed out he needed a job because he had no money. Tuggy Tug announced that any day now he would be receiving income support. Anita looked at her computer and made a tutting sound. He was not due for income support because he had not replied to the letter they had sent out asking what course he was attending. 'It's called a learning agreement,' she said brightly.

'But he has trouble reading,' I said, 'let alone replying to official letters.' Had his social worker not helped him? Surely it was a routine task for a social worker? Tuggy Tug looked at me blankly.

'Well,' she said, 'he never provided the information, so they closed his case down.' Her eyes remained on the screen. 'At the moment he owes £1,499.50 in rent arrears.'

I recalled the series of mean rooms Tuggy Tug had called

home since I had known him. He was a child from care. How could he possibly owe such a large sum? She shrugged. Housing was meant to pay his rent but he had never made a claim. So this was a case of one government department owing another? Well yes, she conceded, but Tuggy Tug had to pay it.

'I told you Harry, I told you,' said Tuggy Tug. 'If you get a nice-paid job you have to pay every pound you earn back to the government.' He had indeed told me this on the way to the job centre. I had not understood or believed him.

Anita announced that a specialised 18–24 team helped young men like Tuggy Tug. First he had to sign on to Jobseeker's Allowance. She gave us a number to ring.

As we walked out Tuggy Tug dug Lips in the arm. 'Did you see Gits? It was Gits! Man's slipping that's what I tell you. He's slipping if he's here on a Friday afternoon.' Only losers who could not make money on the road signed on, he said. That was why he did not want to be seen in the place.

Feeling in need of a break, we bought cartons of juice and retreated to the car. Tuggy Tug complained like a small boy. He wanted to be off. He had things to do. 'I am missing out on deals. I got BlackBerries to sell.' We rang the number.

He had reason to complain, as we soon discovered. Signing on for Jobseeker's Allowance is no easy matter. The process took over an hour and required all our expertise. By himself Tuggy Tug would have failed at the third question. 'What's your title please,' asked the man at the other end. Tuggy Tug looked wildly at me. I told him. 'Oh that's what he's pushin' at,' he grumbled. Swagger reached over and switched on speakerphone.

Tuggy Tug then stumbled over the spelling of his name. It contained a lot of 'p's and 'b's. When the man spelt it back using Papa, Bravo, Tuggy Tug was bewildered. He had never heard that terminology before.

The questions went on. 'Are you involved in any industrial action?' 'Are you needed in court?' We paused. Was he? When had he left Feltham? Tuggy Tug was uncertain. Dates barely figured in his life.

Why had he not started his claim before? He mumbled, 'Trying to get myself back on my feet,' then looked at us for inspiration. It was a bit like playing *Who Wants to Be a Millionaire?* – only for less money. What was he doing now? Prompted by Swagger, he replied, spending time with probation and his social worker. I had my own question. Why had neither of these two individuals brought him to the job centre? Why had it been left to me?

How have you supported yourself? This threw us. Street robbery and drug dealing was hardly the right answer. Smalls whispered, 'Family,' Lips came up with 'social worker' and Swagger added 'crisis loan'. It was a question of finding the correct jargon. Reality had nothing to do with it, nor did Tuggy Tug's plight. The state has failed to notice that young men like Tuggy Tug do not even know enough to sign on.

At this point, half an hour into the questions, authority announced his shift was over. We should call back later. I grabbed the phone and exploded. I was a taxpayer, I said, and expected a better service. The man hung up. Tuggy Tug shook his head. 'I told you this place fair gives you a headache. That's why me and the others do the robbin', innit. We don't like coming here. None of us have ever signed on.' He paused to finish his orange juice. 'You ought to go on one of them anger management courses,' he added kindly.

A woman now rang but she was pickier. She refused the use of the speakerphone and banned the communal answering of questions. Almost immediately Tuggy Tug got into difficulties. Who was paying his rent arrears and council tax? she asked. Good question, I said, we all wanted to know that. Swagger, forgetting his own anger management course, now seized the phone. 'He's only eighteen,' he said. 'He's got no savings, no mortgage, no bank account and no pension. He's got flipping nothing.'

'Stupid, ridiculous questions,' said Swagger to us but he went on answering them. I now decided we needed to eat. We retreated to Nando's and ordered chicken with coleslaw and chips – Swagger still answering the questions on Tuggy Tug's behalf.

As we waited for the food, Lips, who as usual had refused to take off his hat and anorak, asked Swagger, 'What type of guy were you in the camps [prison]?' Swagger handed back my phone after finally finishing. He explained that he had spent a lot of time in segregation, 'I did not take shit from the guards.' He had been moved to fifteen prisons in four and a half years. 'There was a lot of fighting, people taking liberties.' Lips had three older brothers all in prison. He nodded. 'That's the nature in the camps,' he said. I asked if he expected to go to prison. 'Obviously it's what you do,' he said.

His mother blamed the schools for what had happened to her three oldest sons. Desperate, she had sent Lips to Jamaica for a strict, old-fashioned education. But times had changed. Lips explained, 'It's worse there. A girl I hung around with got shot sixteen times. Kids carried bare guns and ratchet knives to school.' So his mother brought him back.

Tuggy Tug looked at his plate piled high with chicken bones. 'This meal! That was justice man,' he announced. At the door the boys paused and checked up and down the road before stepping out. 'Back to reality,' said Tuggy Tug as if the afternoon, the job centre and the chicken had all been a dreamlike interlude.

After they left, Swagger and I had a cappuccino. He was bitter. 'It needed all five of us to deal with the social.' He pointed out Tuggy Tug and the others were not even educated enough to get help from the state. 'And he has been in the system all his life!'

He stirred his coffee angrily. 'Last week I saw that same woman. I was in the same position as Tuggy Tug, trying to get my benefits sorted out. No one understands them. I had to wait five hours to get an emergency cheque signed and I missed my work experience. This week I'm back as a mentor.' He shook his head. 'Madness,' he said, 'madness.'

Swagger's anger dismayed me. With his grace and smile, he had appeared to trip lightly through the realities that destroyed others. When I first knew him, he was always cheerful. 'You all right mate?' he would call out in the street; or throw an arm around an old lady before carrying her bags. The magical and the bizarre were commonplace for Swagger. The week before in a hospital lift, he had bumped into the fashion designer Vivienne Westwood. By the time they got out, she had offered him a modelling job. On the way to the boys that day, he had introduced me to an old school friend. Dressed in white satin and hung with platinum chains, Sweets was considered too dangerous for the police to accost without armed back-up – even for the minor parking offence he had just committed. Swagger greeted him with a joke and an invitation to tea later. And Sweets's carnivorous face had melted.

Back always arched, head gleaming, Swagger approached the world as a delightful dancing partner who required only his warmth to put on a good display. I had never worried about Swagger's future.

Now I glimpsed another side to Swagger's life. Asking him to come to the job centre had been a mistake. This was where he lined up every week and got no help. Like Tuggy Tug, he struggled to turn attributes into an income. I was insisting he help Tuggy Tug achieve what he was failing to achieve himself.

The next day I was due to attend a seminar in the House of

Commons on black fatherhood. Instead I drove down for the next stage in getting Tuggy Tug a job. First I had to find him. There followed the usual flurry of calls. 'I am just there, Harry,' he kept on reassuring me, 'you are goin' to see me coming round the corner in a hot minute.'

Finally he arrived. He was late, he explained, because he had been picking up his washing. He was very upset. At four that morning water had suddenly gushed from the ceiling into his room. He had leapt out of bed to unplug his TV. His bedding and his clothes had all been soaked. He had forgotten to bring the two proofs of identity the job centre required. So we returned to his hostel – still the one managed by the South African couple. When the wife answered the intercom, Tuggy Tug shouted about the leak. The husband flew out, again in his homewear of shorts and vest, and shouted back, 'Don't be rude to my wife.' Still arguing, they went upstairs to look at the damage.

Later Tuggy Tug and I found ourselves on a bright green sofa on the third floor of the job centre. The cheerful upholstery did not make up for the fact that we had sat there a long time. Opposite us fewer than half of the advisers were actually interviewing people. The rest stared at their computers or chatted on the telephone. Tuggy Tug was not happy. No other young black men were waiting.

Tuggy Tug pointed to one of the advisers, a woman with huge bosoms, a round face and short limp hair. He said, 'I know she liked Smalls. She always try to help him.' What form had this taken? In order to keep Smalls off the street and out of trouble, she drew out his appointments – just a little bit longer. That was it? Tuggy Tug shrugged. Compared to the normal indifference, it seemed a lot.

Swagger now arrived. To emphasise his mentor status, he had dressed in a new pale blue jacket, a blue shirt and matching trainers. His jeans were patched with a piece of embroidered orange silk. Tuggy Tug and I eyed him in admiration. Tuggy Tug said, 'You look fly [good], fam.'

Finally a large man with untidy hair called Dave called us over – but only to go through the questions we had answered the day before. Could Tuggy Tug's benefit claim be backdated in order to wipe off his housing debt? Swagger asked. I was confused. We seemed to have wandered off into an impenetrable tangle of claims and benefits. Where were we, I wanted to know, in the process of getting him a job? Everyone looked at me in surprise. I had failed to grasp that job centres are not about jobs. They are about benefits.

I now got out my notepad to take down Dave's response and get the process clear in my mind. Dave said cheerfully, 'Nobody stands a cat in hell's chance of getting a benefit backdated. They have skinned off all the excuses for backdating but they still provide a form for you to fill in.' He pushed over a booklet. Swagger and I pointed out that he had no money. How was he supposed to pay his rent, let alone the debt? Dave nodded. 'I would have thought that was common sense,' he agreed, then added, 'you might get a human response out of them but, mind you, I am not promising.'

Swagger suggested a crisis loan. I had no idea what that was. Tuggy Tug said, 'You are going to be on the phone ten hours before anyone pick up, trust me fam.' Swagger dialled the number on my mobile. It was answered immediately. Delighted, Tuggy Tug went off with my phone to apply.

Swagger leaned on Dave's desk and started to fill in the form for a backdated application. He wrote slowly, insisting on getting everything right, half sounding out the words. Most he misread or misspelt. I got impatient, almost angry. I was shocked to see someone so eloquent beached by the written word. On he plodded and his doggedness on Tuggy Tug's behalf now broke my heart. He did not seem to understand that the form was pointless.

To distract myself, I turned back to Dave. What about training and a job – the reason, after all, we were there? The brochure downstairs had promised a 'personal adviser' who 'will work with customers to create a personalised back to work plan with an expanding menu of support'.

Dave looked at me pityingly. 'No one has a rat's-arse chance of getting a job here,' he said. 'You are not dealing with a system that is here to help. Anyone not prepared to jump through the hoops, they blow away at the slightest excuse.' He nodded at the advisers busy behind their computers. 'They don't care, you see. If you don't play the game, they got no sense of humour. If he doesn't play, and he won't being the type of young man that he is, they will brush him off and give him short shrift. One infraction and they will refuse to see him again.'

Surely, in this target-driven culture, a job centre had a target for getting Neets like Tuggy Tug into training and work? Dave said, 'They don't have to prove they get anyone a job.'

What about that expanding menu of support? What about training schemes that led to a job?

'They are just there to churn the figures,' he said. 'The training is useless. They don't lead to a job that will pay a sustainable wage. They do not last long enough to do any good.' He explained it was all about massaging the Neet figures in order to make them politically acceptable. On this he and Tuggy Tug did at least agree. Tuggy Tug had complained that he and his friends had already done 'All those little courses that get you nowhere.'

Dave glanced down at the form Swagger was still painfully filling in. Tuggy Tug returned, grunted at us then wandered out for a smoke. Dave watched him then went on, 'We do represent a problem for a lot of young people – especially young men like himself. He is his own worst enemy at the moment. They need something like a life course.' He shook his head. 'I am old, tired and cynical now but when I was growing up I would go down the local pub. There some grown-up man would thump anyone like me who put a foot out of line.'

He grew thoughtful. I waited, hoping he was coming up with a plan. Finally he said, 'There is a desk on the ground floor, at the same spot as this. There they find work for people who suffer from a mental or physical disability. Is he like that for medical reasons? Is he, you know, mentally deficient?'

I was so shocked I just stared at Dave. Then I looked to Swagger but he was still struggling with the pointless form. Here was a young man who we both found bright and engaging being dismissed as mentally not all there. 'Nothing is wrong with him,' I finally said. 'He has just been brought up by the state.'

Once again Swagger, Tuggy Tug and I found ourselves waiting on the cheerful green sofa. 'I hate this place,' I said to Tuggy Tug. He shrugged. 'You have no choice, you get me, but to sit down here to get a little money.' Later I heard him remark to Swagger, 'She's not silly. Like every day she comes down here and learns something new. She's learning mad fast. She's learning quite a lot now.'

Finally I got up and walked over to the lady who had helped Smalls. She glanced at my expression. 'Got to go,' she said and put down the phone. We sat in front of her and she handed Tuggy Tug a test. He had to look at a job application then answer questions. He did not do well. Slowly, with no sense of urgency, she put together a series of forms and asked him to sign. Tuggy Tug suddenly sat up. 'Is this "signing on"?' he asked. 'Blud I am signing on. I am signing on,' he exclaimed excitedly.

This was the only rite of passage he knew. The only rite of passage he was allowed.

He could not sign his name properly. He just wrote his first name in childish letters.

All three of us had now turned truculent. Swagger was rubbing his head and sighing. Tuggy Tug started to doodle on one of the job centre's glossy leaflets. He drew black squares over the smiling ethnic faces on the front cover. These he filled in with increasing violence until his pen broke right through. 'Don't mark my desk,' said the woman.

She asked about my children and showed me a photograph of her teenage son. He was fifteen, suffered from autism and was doing twelve GCSEs. I was taken aback. My son had managed eleven. 'Yes,' she went on, 'he loves cooking and wants to go into catering.' Not Oxford or Cambridge? I asked. She looked puzzled. 'A catering NVQ counts as six GCSEs,' she explained. She told Tuggy Tug he would go on receiving benefits as long as he turned up every week and wrote down two jobs that he had tried for.

'But what about actually getting him a job?' I said. That was for tomorrow and the 18–24 team.

I got stuck in traffic and missed the interview. Tuggy Tug complained to Swagger, 'And she is telling me to be a hundred per cent!' I was astonished to learn that he had gone on his own to the job centre and seen the woman from the 18–24 team. This was a big step forward. I asked what she had done for him. Tuggy Tug shrugged. She had directed him to a government website. 'That's it,' I exclaimed, 'we have signed you on, gone through three days in that place for a website address? What about a job? What about training or finding what you might be good at?' Tuggy Tug shook his head. There had been nothing like that. 'I told you Harry,' he said.

Out on Streatham High Street the clouds had cleared and the sun was shining. It was the first truly warm day of summer. Tuggy

Tug had his usual reaction to good weather. He looked around and pulled his hood up. 'Everyone's on the road,' he said grimly.

Tuggy Tug now announced he needed to open a bank account. His father had been in touch and was offering to send him money. We walked up and down Streatham High Street visiting banks. One appeared promising until they asked for two proofs of identity. Tuggy Tug pulled out what he had provided the job centre – his passport and a letter from court demanding his attendance. This second piece of paper did not satisfy the woman. 'But it's from a government department,' I pointed out. 'And it's got his name and address.'

Tuggy Tug began to shout at the woman, his face contorted, with a sudden surge of aggression. I dragged him away and told him off. That would get him nowhere. He had to smile and be polite.

I insisted we go to an Internet café and search for the website 'Backing Young Britain' provided by the lady from the 18–24 team. Unlike the job centre, the café was efficient, cheap and run by a helpful Asian. No amount of help could make up for the fact that Tuggy Tug did not have a clue how to use a computer beyond looking at Facebook. He certainly did not know how to find the website or set up the account it now demanded.

The website made the same inflated promises as the job centre. It guaranteed thousands of jobs, work experience and apprenticeships. Who wrote these? I wondered. Were they cynical or just ignorant?

Defeated by the website, Tuggy Tug now left to try out his smile on a bank. I searched under the site's categories. I started with sales. '1866 opportunities match your criteria,' exclaimed the website. I entered Streatham but the site did not recognise the area. So I reverted to South London. Here only one retail opportunity existed in the whole of South London – as a shop assistant in Basildon. I now tried catering: no opportunities in South London. Construction: no jobs in the whole of London. I then tried under manufacturing and horticulture: no opportunities. The other categories, accountancy, banking, finance, insurance, were way beyond Tuggy Tug.

In despair, I rang a man I had met at a party and who owned a string of restaurants across London. Catering did not require qualifications. It seemed just the ticket. Did he advertise jobs at the job centre? He burst out laughing. Of course not, he said. He did not employ anyone English: 'anyone who has gone through the English state school system. Look on Gumtree, that's where we get our workers. They are all foreign. Mexicans are the flavour this week.' How come Mexicans were getting jobs in restaurants but not Tuggy Tug? He did not know and was not interested.

Teenage boys like Tuggy Tug disengage from society for a reason. They see nothing in it for them. And in this they are quite right. Semi-literate, in competition with skilled and motivated immigrants, they are not qualified for well-paid jobs and the benefit system excludes them from taking low-paid work as a first step to something better. More and more young men find it difficult to take those first steps to an independent adult existence. Smalls described his despair at the prospect of a lifetime dependent on benefits. He saw his future clearly: 'I know men of forty doing nothing but drink and drugs all day. I don't blame them.' He shook his head angrily. 'But it's too early for me. I don't want to be beat like that.' I said Swagger was nearly forty. He was turning his life around. Smalls just looked at me.

A year later I found myself in a meeting with two civil servants from the Department for Work and Pensions. I described my experience. They assured me that was not meant to happen. How did they measure job centres? They said, 'Well, when we visit, everyone is terribly enthusiastic.' They paused; one woman frowned. She admitted they did not have an internal league table to compare one job centre to another. They did not even know the numbers of people each job centre got into work. It is rather like Tesco running its business without checking if any of its stores have ever actually sold a single item.

Dave had spoken the truth. Job centre staff are under no pressure to find work for anyone. They can spend the day chatting on the phone, handing out forms, messing up lives and no one knows or cares.

I urged the civil servants, pleasant and intelligent people, to visit a job centre with one of my young men. They looked embarrassed. Perhaps I could bring Tuggy Tug and Smalls to give evidence? I never heard from them.

Back on the street, I spotted Swagger in a cake shop. He had been applying for a job working on a railway station platform. It had meant filling in a twenty-page form online. A Pole had told him about the work. 'He seems to have no trouble with those forms,' said Swagger gloomily. He had made two attempts and was now having a break. Foreigners seem so motivated, I remarked. Swagger snorted. 'Of course they are. They work here but look at what they buy back home! I seen it on the telly, big houses and nice gardens. That's motivating, that is. If I work on a platform for the minimum wage I am never going to get no big house and garden ever – unless I move to the Third World. All I get is a headache, less money than on benefits and a summons to court for rent arrears.'

Tuggy Tug burst in and danced up to the display of cakes. 'Swagger, Swagger,' he shouted – he always called out Swagger's name when he was excited – 'are you watchin' those cakes blud? Swagger those cake look a dream!' I said I had turned into an anarchist. 'See,' said Swagger. 'What we been telling you.' They had but I had not believed them. 'Next you will be robbin' security vans like me,' said Swagger. Tuggy Tug, eating through a slice of cake, considered the day a success. The smile had worked. He had opened a bank account and got a crisis loan of £30. 'You are on the job when you want to be,' said Swagger in admiration.

Afterwards we took him back to his hostel. He stared around disconsolately. There was a smell of damp from the early morning flood. His TV would not turn on. He looked at what I had bought him, two towels and a book on how to succeed at business. He showed me his plastic bag full of papers. Social worker after social worker wrote to introduce themselves. A few months later there followed a second letter. It announced either that they had gone on sick leave or had joined a new team with an impressive title. 'I never get to see them,' grumbled Tuggy Tug. He appeared to be no more than a distraction in the ritual of bureaucratic advancement or retirement.

At the bottom of the bag, I retrieved letters from Wandsworth Council demanding payment of his rent arrears. They warned they would 'instigate legal proceedings'. He should immediately provide the necessary information. 'Without this information you cannot receive Housing Benefit and the debt will be classified as yours.' They had helpfully provided a summary of his various hostels and what he owed for each of them.

I sat down on the wet bed. My head ached. How was he ever to clear this debt? How had he been allowed to get into debt in the first place? Why had none of those social workers done something to help him? How many other young men were in the same position? No wonder he and his friends were so reluctant to step into the job centre.

The civil servants had talked excitedly of 'delivering initiatives' through job centres. They never thought to ask young men like Tuggy Tug their views. And so their plans were doomed to failure at great cost to the young men and to the rest of us, the taxpayers. I doubted they even understood why.

The state had ensnared Tuggy Tug, and even Swagger and I had been unable to set him free. We had achieved nothing in three days – apart from finding a good cake shop.

Tuggy Tug now pulled out a second plastic bag. This one, however, was filled not with demands from the state but pencil sketches done by an older brother while in prison. Tuggy Tug's brother lacked technique but he knew how to convey anger, boredom and passion. Tuggy Tug showed me a fight: 'Look at them eyes, blud. Yeah and see that one with the knife.' I looked closer at what appeared to be a sharpened toothbrush. 'He's goin' in. He's goin' to get his knife game on.' He pushed them into my hands. 'Take them Harry. I want you to have them.'

He turned to Swagger and they began to joke about a friend of Swagger's who grew skunk in his hanging wardrobe and had been robbed the night before by two young men the same age as Tuggy Tug. For the first time I did not disapprove. I was on their side. Against the bulwark of bureaucracy, their ebullience now took on a miraculous light.

Twenty

The visit to the job centre at least had inspired Swagger to make another attempt at a career. He now tried voluntary work with a charity. Voluntary work, they promised, might lead to a full-time job. It took barely a month for euphoria to once again give way to disillusion. And as before he wanted me to come down and see what was really going on. 'They're as bad as the job centre,' he said in disgust.

The charity laid on courses to prepare young people for work. One young man on the course had got to Swagger. Hubert was eighteen and the same age as Tuggy Tug but he was well-spoken and had a clutch of GCSEs. Swagger was astonished that Hubert was on the course at all. The rest of the young people were illiterate, drug dealers or crackheads. One girl stole a computer and smashed up two classrooms. 'Them little kids are mash up,' Swagger said.

The week-long course had been a humiliating experience for Hubert. The others assumed that Hubert was taking the piss out of them. He had to stand up and formally apologise to the group – apologise, in essence, for being educated and articulate. He had to explain that this was the way he spoke and that he was not trying to belittle them.

Hubert was on the course because the charity that ran the hostel where he was staying had insisted he attend. Swagger said, 'It's not just gang members that get let down.' The charity offered accommodation and education. Swagger wanted me to meet Hubert and see the work of the charity from his point of view.

Hubert hurried up to us in the lobby. He was tall, with a narrow face and hands that flapped at his surroundings or dived into his pockets like a pair of angry birds. I looked around, impressed. The lobby in this hostel was a world away from those inhabited by Tuggy Tug and Mash. It was large, freshly decorated and boasted four new computers on elegant glass consoles. Hubert was not a young man to bother with small talk. He saw my expression. Bitterness burned off him as he put me right. 'This place is a rip-off,' he declared. He pointed to the computers: 'State-of-the-art? They're just to show visitors. Half of the time the staff shut off the Internet. The other half they block off websites for no reason.' It was, for example, impossible for him to do a job search.

His room was in stark contrast to the lobby. He showed me the peeling walls, the filthy carpet, the shower with its trickle of water, the single bare light bulb and the window that never closed. Everything was cheap and nasty when it would have taken so little to make it pleasant. 'They made all sorts of promises at first,' recalled Hubert. They promised to paint the place, provide a new carpet and a Starter Pack. When nothing happened and no Starter Pack appeared, 'I used to go every day to complain,' said Hubert, 'every day.' The manager told him there was a back-log. Hubert discovered the backlog had lasted seven years. 'They couldn't even provide a mop and bucket to keep the place clean.'

A week before, his cooker had blown up. 'I warned them it would,' he said. He had nothing to put out the fire. The fire extinguisher was empty and the emergency blanket missing. In the end he had grabbed a pot and banged it over the flames. 'I didn't want it destroying my things,' he said. He went on, 'If it's not an emergency, it takes months to get anything fixed. If it is an emergency, it still takes months.'

He admitted grudgingly they had started to decorate: 'But it's the staff rooms they are doing up first.'

Things 'had gone sour' between Hubert and his foster mother when he was twelve. Shortly afterwards his brother, to whom he was close, died. Hubert had gone through a bad time and dropped out of college. Now he was eager to resume his education and get a job.

He wanted social services to find him a flat. In order to get the referrals from the hostel for that to happen, 'you have to interact with the courses offered by the hostel otherwise they don't let you out'. This gave him little time for job-hunting. In fact getting a job would land him in difficulties. It would put a halt to the all-important 'interacting with courses' and his plans to move out. He said of the courses, 'That's all management here seems to care about.'

The problem was that most of the courses were 'the basic of the basics', designed for the barely literate. 'They have nothing at my level.' He finished the IT course with ease but then he already had one GCSE for IT – something his key worker had ignored. The IT teacher offered to teach him to a higher level but the manager said they lacked the funds. Instead he praised Hubert for his intelligence. Hubert dismissed this as 'patronising'. He said bitterly, 'Don't tell me I am clever just because I know how to use a knife and fork. That's insulting.'

He had had four support and development workers in two months and 'one stress after the next with the staff'. He conducted a running battle with his key worker. 'I don't like him. He is useless and he doesn't listen to a word I have to say.' But then Hubert, I suspected, was a great deal brighter than his key worker. Once a week he received counselling for his brother's death and his mother's and foster mother's rejection of him. 'A waste of time,' remarked Hubert. His counsellor spent the first fifteen minutes of a half-hour session smoking outside. When Hubert remonstrated, he stubbed out his cigarette, saying, 'Well, I can still do you in fifteen minutes.'

The morning of my visit his key worker had suggested a cookery course. Hubert said, 'I think he's being spiteful.'

The charity's low expectations distressed him. 'They don't promote things that actually help you. They think I am very smart so that's it, I don't need to do more.'

The charity might be failing Hubert but they still made good use of him. One morning he was invited to come downstairs and sign up for a photography course. Hubert arrived in the lobby to find it full of smartly dressed men and women. The manager apologised. He had just missed the sign-on. Instead, would he mind meeting a government minister and various wealthy sponsors? Hubert, black, neatly dressed and articulate, pushed all the right buttons. Everyone lined up to shake his hand and be photographed with him. The next time the manager wanted to show him off, 'I refused.' He never did get to find out about the photography course.

His experience of the charity coming so soon after his other problems, together with the sense that his future was shrivelling up in front of him, left Hubert in despair. 'What next will they do to me?' he demanded. 'I am surprised when I moved in here there weren't some ropes and a razor laid out on the floor waiting for me.'

Hubert said he wanted us to meet his friend. Maybe Swagger could help him as well?

I had thought Hubert's room might have been a one-off. In an identical room down to the bare light bulb, Gabriel, sixteen years old and white with soft, sad, dope-filled eyes, was slumped on his bed. 'My life has been horrible,' he said in a low voice. His mother had recently died. His stepfather had turned him out after the funeral. 'I had lived with my stepdad for thirteen years but he gave me up when my mum died.' Had he wanted to come here? 'I had no choice. My local authority put me here.'

The room was bare except for some dirty clothes and a torn poster on the floor. A banana skin lay on the desk, which had lost a drawer and a leg. Gabriel showed me all he had left from his previous life – two crumpled-up photographs. In one his mother, round-faced and laughing, had thrown her arms around him and his two small stepsisters. The other showed him aged seven in a playground clutching the hand of a girl a few years younger in shorts and a frilly top. This was his sister, who had also died. Otherwise the room was empty of anything personal. 'Well things get nicked,' he said matter-of-fact. As well as weed, Gabriel took medication, 'for all the sad stuff in my head'.

Hubert explained that Gabriel received both disability and bereavement allowance. This left him comparatively well off. 'He should get a little money every day,' said Hubert, 'so it doesn't all go on drugs. His key worker is meant to do that. But then his key worker don't turn up or goes off sick and Gabriel is left with nothing.' Hubert believed the staff were stealing money from Gabriel. Gabriel glanced admiringly at Hubert. 'He tells it how it is,' he said. 'He's my only friend.'

The last time staff had failed to give Gabriel his allowance, he had picked up a fire extinguisher and smashed the place up. Gabriel looked sheepish. 'I got hungry,' he said. I asked about loneliness. His eyes filled with tears and he had to look away.

The place was also dangerous. The two boys were afraid of their neighbours. Gabriel went on, 'It's a madhouse here.'

Hubert agreed. 'If you basically say the wrong thing to the wrong person then it's all over for you.' He had tried complaining to the staff about the noise from the other rooms but 'they do nothing about it. They just go through the procedure. "Fill in the form and drop it in the box," they say.'

Hubert was ticking off to Swagger the number of people responsible for him and Gabriel, social workers, key workers, counsellors, advisers. 'We are just a job to them,' Hubert said.

Despite the large numbers of staff, no one cooked them breakfast in the morning or asked how their day had gone in the evening.

Gabriel said, 'It's very easy to get yourself in shit and you can't get out of it.' He apologised, smiled dreamily and slumped back on his bed.

I looked around that grim little room overwhelmed. I thought of all the boys I had interviewed and befriended and all with the same story. Something had happened to them when they were too young: abuse, neglect or the death of a sibling or a parent. They had begun to act up. Everyone reacted to the behaviour. No one asked why they were behaving badly in the first place or tried to do something about it. 'It's just a can of worms I don't have time to deal with,' said one social worker to me.

So here they are, providing jobs for large numbers of people as their lives waste away. They are the pet everyone has got bored of – lonely, hungry and dangerous.

Swagger tried to get his charity to help. 'They say you have to set boundaries,' he sighed, but Swagger did not know the meaning of the word. He wanted to change Hubert and Gabriel's lives rather than just secure next year's funding. 'I let the boys down,' he said. 'And imagine this, Harry, the boys weren't upset. They did not expect any different.' Shortly afterwards, the charity, tired of his pestering, suggested he might volunteer elsewhere.

It no longer surprised me that Tuggy Tug saw state and charity as one and the same; or that he wanted nothing to do with either. I had even begun to admire him for it.

Twenty-one

Then suddenly, just like that, I cracked the problem. I discovered the Skills Academy, a government organisation that offered jobs at £150 a week. What made these jobs special was that the £150 came clear of tax. It also did not affect housing benefit. It was miraculous. All our problems seemed solved. First the boys had to sign on. I told Lips to get down to the job centre. Tuggy Tug admitted he had not actually been back since our visit but I decided to treat this as a formality. I told him to meet me at the Tickle Me Café. He arrived with Lips and Belly, Tuggy Tug's cousin, all, in their eagerness, on time. The bored servers for once had not run out of muffins or hot chocolate.

Lips, his hat pulled low over his braids, his anorak zipped up over his chin despite the spring weather, was unsure. He asked Tuggy Tug, 'Do you reckon you'll be able to hold down this job if you get it?'

'If I can see that it helps,' said Tuggy Tug and turned to Belly. 'I could get you a job you know that?' he went on. 'You have to be in the job centre to get it. It's a bill fifty a week yeah. No taxes so you get a whole hundred and fifty a week.' On top of that, 'This job proper opens doors like.'

Did he know what he was supposed to do? asked Belly.

'No not yet, not until we get there fam. That's how it is fam.'

Lips's narrow face broke open in a rare smile. He unzipped the top few inches of his anorak and said, 'I'm in. I wanna see what this is about.'

'I'm doing it fam, you get me?' Tuggy Tug announced, talking through a mouthful of muffin. He explained, 'This is all like ends and that [means to an end] you get me?' He emphasised the word 'ends' as if he were about to hit it. He went on, 'These jobs take place in sports arenas and that. Like gym things and them types of things.' These jobs were not 'normal dead garden and all office work and none of that. Sports, innit. Might keep cool if man works with this yeah he's due to get a job for the Olympics and that.'

Sometime in the last few months Tuggy Tug had stopped referring to himself as 'boy' and now talked about 'man'. The other morning he had proclaimed, 'Man ain't feelin' these cockroaches cotchin' [hanging out] on my bedroom floor.'

Tuggy Tug continued lecturing the others, one of his favourite occupations. 'Yeah cos these people they've got the links and that. One little dead side job man can get you . . . you get me. What them call dead is big, very big fam. You know steward, them man what just hand out those little flyers. Big man, getting cake blud. A bill fifty man . . .'

Belly, a serious young man in his mid-twenties who was determined to get on despite a firearms offence, leant forward. 'See when you get links like this bruv,' he said to Tuggy Tug, nodding at me, 'suck it to the fullest bruv, you get me? Don't give up fam. Don't give up. If I see you in the hood next year I will tell you fam you flopped me yeah. You hear me? I'll rub it in fam. You hear me I'll rub it in fam. Don't flop them opportunities fam.'

I informed the Skills Academy I was now bringing not one hoodie but three. I had to keep ringing as the list grew longer. As soon as news spread of the deal, £150 and housing benefit, I got more and more calls starting with a brisk 'I hear you are the jobs lady.' The moment the sums made sense, the moment they could make something clear of benefits, they were on to it. But

I discovered the Skills Academy too late. Before the boys could take up the jobs, it was abolished after the 2010 election.

The result was predictable. A month after we heard the news about the Skills Academy, Tuggy Tug was arrested. I rang Lips. Tuggy Tug was already out and round at Lips's flat. He had been found not guilty. He had no money and nowhere to stay. All his clothes were in something called 'lock-up'. He said, 'The police and that they took all my money.' 'That's outrageous,' I said. Without thinking, my sympathies were now wholly with him.

'Don't say that Harry man,' Tuggy Tug begged, 'I am tryin' not to think like that because it makes me mad. I can't even go to housing because I am not allowed in the area. I got nothing to change into. Five days later I am in the same clothes I went to jail wearin'. I got no choice.'

He was staying the night with Lips. I sent round a pizza. They were very pleased. Lips got on the phone to ask for an order of strawberry ice cream. I promised to come down on Friday and get his clothes out of lock-up – another baffling institution, I presumed.

I never did find out about lock-up. That weekend I went to stay with friends in the countryside. I was standing in a garden centre choosing a rose bush when I got the message, the first Tuggy Tug had ever left on my phone. 'Harry I am in prison. I will call in a hot minute.' At eighteen Tuggy Tug had now graduated to 'big man's prison'. The next time he called, I was so flustered that I dropped the phone. He left his prison number and the name of the prison where he was on remand. At the end of the message his voice turned desperate: 'So why aren't you pickin' up your phone Harry?'

Swagger discovered Tuggy Tug had been detained for street robbery. Lips was with him but kept quiet and the police let him go. Tuggy Tug mouthed off and was arrested.

I knew Tuggy Tug deserved to be in prison. But my heart sank. He had just entered an institution branded a costly failure even by the government. It particularly fails young short-term prisoners like Tuggy Tug. Three-quarters of them reoffend within two years of getting out. This first sentence promised to confirm him into a lifetime of crime. Like half of all young prisoners, he had come out of the care system. Now he had graduated from one expensive and failing institution into another. Our time together had merely been an interlude. His life had resumed its depressing trajectory.

The news hit Swagger hard. He said on the phone to me as he walked down Tulse Hill, 'I am upset, Harry man. First time in big-man prison. I know what he'll be going through. He'll be lying in his cell saying to the summer sky, "Get dark, get dark. Everyone's outside enjoying themselves and I am in a hot, stuffy cell."' Swagger called out to greet a friend then went on, 'He'll be thinking of everything we said. He'll be bullied and disciplined in all different ways.'

I heard a siren in his distance. In my background he heard Radio 4. Someone was describing a stroll in the countryside. He remarked he had listened to Radio 4 in prison. 'You lie down in your cell and you 'ear all those stories. You see everything they say. The guard come in and is amazed you are not listening to hip hop.' He sighed. 'Tuggy Tug, man, why have you done this to me? I am an emotional man,' he added. Then I heard him joking with someone in the petrol station as he bought a packet of ten cigarettes. He took up again with me. 'Yeah Harry man. Those little boys get people to care and then they can't deal with it.'

At first it seemed every aspect of the prison was a punishment, right down to the visitors' booking line which remained obstinately engaged. I looked at the prison website. It stressed the importance of visits. I tried the main switchboard. No, it was not broken, said the operator, just busy. 'It's a terrible system,' she added. A recorded voice informed me that number was unavailable 'at present' and cut off. Swagger shook his head and said of Tuggy Tug, 'He's got a mouth on him. They'll be taking him down in all different ways. And he's only little.'

I began to ring five to ten times a day. After four days a woman picked up. My elation was short-lived. She denied all knowledge of Tuggy Tug. Sometimes they were turned away at the gate, she added, and bussed elsewhere. No, she had no idea where he might be.

I called Lips to see if he knew which prison Tuggy Tug was in. It was 11.30 a.m.; he was just waking up and unable to give me an answer. 'Give me a hot minute,' he begged. He told me Tuggy Tug had moved to Feltham. I tried calling there but once again they refused to give me any information.

I was at a conference on welfare reform in Westminster when Swagger texted me. He had received a letter from Tuggy Tug. In relief I escaped at the coffee break to call him. I was feeling more and more uncomfortable at such events. I did not recognise the world of poverty and disadvantage the speakers described. They always called for more money and more professional help – and finished by blaming, in sorrowful tones, poor backgrounds and bad parenting. None of them ever mentioned their own role, the role of the state.

Swagger read the letter out over the phone in his halting read-aloud voice. Tuggy Tug was still mouthing off. He wanted to sue social services because 'All they have done is sell me false dreams.' He asked us to visit him and bring a prayer mat, shower slippers and three or four hoodies without a hood. Finally he finished, 'As you and Swagger are the only people who write to me so if you forget about me thank you coz I'll never forget u r betta tan any 1 I no its like u r the only 1 ho care. All I want is a job so I can

follow my dreams and become apart of this life and that is real.'
Suddenly the vast room in which I was standing with its columns
and painted ceiling and the people around me murmuring over
their coffee and exchanging business cards shook and collapsed
like a backdrop after the play is over. 'Are you there?' demanded
Swagger. 'Ah don't get all mashed up, Harry man. That's just
prison talk.'

The next day I heard from Tuggy Tug's solicitor. Tuggy Tug
had told him to tell me about the case. The solicitor said he did
not think there was any point in me finding Tuggy Tug a job. He
had decided to make a clean break and admit to five offences.
The police believed him guilty of fifty to a hundred street robberies.

Later I saw Shaun Bailey at a *Spectator* party. About to become
Big Society Ambassador to the Prime Minister, he was himself the
son of a single mother from a north Kensington estate. I said I
was upset to discover Tuggy Tug guilty of such a large number of
robberies. Shaun smiled. 'But Harriet,' he said, 'he is a gang leader.
Drugs and robberies, that's what gangs do. What did you expect?'

I rang the prison to arrange a visit. This time it took two days
to get through. Once again the woman denied any knowledge of
Tuggy Tug. In desperation I begged her to look again. Surely he
could not just disappear. I felt like a Russian trying to track down
a relative in the Gulag. 'There's nothing here,' she said. 'It is like
he does not exist.'

The next day my two letters to Tuggy Tug were returned without explanation.

Unlike the Gulag, I could write to the prison governor, who
rang me within an hour of getting my letter and apologised for
my 'visitor's experience'. Shortly after, Swagger got through and
arranged a visit. Tuggy Tug had magically appeared inside the
prison.

That was not the end of it. I soon discovered that getting directions was almost as difficult as an answer from the prison visiting line. Google Maps refused to display a route. I tried the AA. Here too I drew a blank. 'A particular road has restricted access.' Prisons, I was learning, exist in a different universe from the rest of us. Swagger announced he had been an inmate at the same prison. He could remember the route from going back and forth to court 'in the sweat box'.

On the way we dropped by Lips's house to pick up clothes for Tuggy Tug. His mother, a kindly woman with large eyes, had Tuggy Tug's possessions stacked in two black bin bags under her kitchen table. Apart from his clothes there were the two books on business I had given him and a copy of the Koran. When I pulled out an iPhone box, Lips and Swagger hurriedly removed it. It was full of weed.

We then discussed which pair of trainers to take to Tuggy Tug. This was no small decision. The soul of the hoodie resides in his trainers. In the end Lips's mother chose a blue pair with high sides in black.

I wondered what the earnest people at my conference would make of her. She was a single mother but she lived in a comfortable flat. There was little sign of social deprivation. She herself was a strong, intelligent woman who wanted the best for her children. She had even sent Lips to Jamaica, so desperate was she that he should have the traditional education her other sons had failed to get from their inner-city schools. She laid the blame for their descent into criminality not on their background but on their schools, the lack of competitive sports to soak up their energy and the absence of jobs. As I left she begged me to find Lips a job and keep him from following his brothers into jail. 'There is nothing for them to do. Nothing,' she said.

The prison was on top of a hill at the end of a windy road. We had got lost many times. There were no signs. We learnt who to ask: young women pushing prams and old men smoking were a good bet. Anyone middle-class, however long they had lived in the area, rarely knew of the prison's existence.

The visitors' centre was outside the prison walls, a large, low room with every nationality and age seated at its round tables. Volunteers staffed it, brisk, kindly women a world away in attitude from those I had encountered in the job centre. But even they could only do so much to explain the baffling system.

We queued to hand over Tuggy Tug's trainers. It was unclear what items we could leave. A notice set a time limit dated from the prisoner's arrival. The difficulties of getting through to the visitors' line meant most of us had missed that. In front of me a respectable middle-aged couple in matching chinos and fleeces were almost in tears. 'But he has to have shower slippers,' they said to the prison officer. Their minds boggled at a life without shower slippers – never mind the soap box and framed family photograph the officer now rejected.

In the loo women were getting ready 'to crank up their men', as Swagger remarked. They slipped into teetering heels, brushed out their long hair, applied lipstick and sprayed on perfume. Some were very young with babies in prams; or pregnant, stomachs pointing from slim bodies through bandagelike dresses or barely covered by brief, off-the-shoulder tops and leggings. A notice on the wall listed clothing deemed inappropriate. None of the girls appeared to have read it. They all eyed me. 'Have you come to see your fella then?' one asked dubiously. Outside I found Swagger chatting to a plump, middle-aged woman. She was married with children but once a month visited her lover who was locked up. None of her family knew. She enjoyed the illicitness, 'and it makes a nice day out', she added.

By the time it came to the mouth search for drugs I opened mine without a murmur.

In the hall where the visits took place, the prison officer looked down his list then pursed his lips. 'Never heard of him. Are you sure he's in this prison?' Beyond, at a low table, grinning fit to burst, sat Tuggy Tug.

Around us male prisoners in their distinguishing yellow vests cradled babies, argued with parents or held girlfriends' hands across the strategically placed coffee tables. At the table next door, two generations of a family from Essex offered a consolatory crisp to their criminal grandfather. A traveller with an elaborate earring and curly hair nodded off as his wife anxiously questioned their son. Across from them black and mixed-race men with prayer beads and tattoos exchanged jokes with a fellow gang member. Earlier, one had removed his prayer shawl to reveal a T-shirt bearing the slogan 'Grind Hard. Keep Faith.'

Among all this I had expected to find Tuggy Tug flattened by a system that had defeated me. We had all underestimated the desperation of his previous existence. Tuggy Tug now glowed with happiness and health.

Yes, as for any boy new to boarding school, the first days had been trying. Three guards had restrained him. He had been put into solitary. Then he had to prove himself to the other inmates. Here he waved his arms about, acting out the confrontation between himself and a bigger assailant. Wham, Tuggy knocked him down for us. He explained, 'My rating was this low before.' His hand hovered just off the floor. He beamed. 'Now it's high, fam.'

That was not his only achievement. He had a job in the kitchen and was doing an NVQ in catering. 'All that time I was trying to find work on the outside,' he said, 'and I get it in prison!'

He was also using the gym. He bent forward so I could feel

his pecs. He described his day with pride – an hour in the gym between eight and nine then down to the kitchen to work, followed by study and a game of ball before bang-up. He had, he said in wonder, started to read books, well, 'comic-like books', he amended.

This new order even extended to his cell. The first night he noticed in disgust the wall was covered 'with old bogeys'. He had managed to persuade a prison officer to have it repainted then charmed polish out of a cleaner to make his floor shine and even an air-freshener for when his cell mate used the toilet. 'It's looking real nice now,' he said with satisfaction. I almost expected an invitation to tea.

He contrasted his ordered and productive days with his old life. Outside he had been afraid all the time. 'Every day was a battle man,' he complained. He had been worried about the police and rival gangs. Home was a 'poxy little room' in a hostel with no cooking facilities. He had no family to miss. He admitted to us he was frequently lonely and nearly always hungry. It was a miserable existence.

Now he wanted for nothing. 'You can live on ten pounds a week here easy,' he explained. He was well fed: 'All this protein,' he said with relish. He smoked the occasional spliff and he even liked the prison officers. He pointed to the massive, Shrek-like men with bald heads dotted around the room. 'They are fair, man. That one' – he nodded at a frankly terrifying individual – 'he's a good officer.' One female officer was doing a lot for him. 'We call her Mum,' he said. She had got him the kitchen job, and on another visit gave up her lunch break to come and chat to me about him. Apart from prison officers, he was also enjoying the companionship. 'There's some good people here,' he said. 'You get to have some wicked conversations.'

His attitude puzzled us until we realised this was Tuggy Tug's first experience of spending time with adult males. His teachers, social workers, probation officer and even the majority of his YOT team were all women. Outside he was on edge, constantly having to prove himself to other young men. After that first fight, the hierarchy of prison life had allowed him to relax. I had never seen him so calm. The food and exercise were having a physical effect. He thrust his jaw out at us. 'Feel that,' he said proudly. I tickled his chin. It was baby-soft. 'There is something there,' persisted Tuggy Tug. Swagger said, 'Prison is turning you into the real big man.'

We spent the two-hour visit planning a job and training. 'Honest fam, I never coming back to prison again,' he assured me. Now Swagger asked what he would do in his first hours out. His eyes lit up. He described how he yearned to see his mates, roll a spliff with them, eat a big pizza and then, to round off the evening, he paused before admitting, 'go robbin' together'. He shook his head in disappointment at the inevitability of his life. 'Back on the road it's the same old same old – like you never been in prison,' he admitted sadly. That is, until he is convicted again.

On the way out I found myself waiting for a door to be unlocked with two girls of about eighteen. They turned to glance back at the roomful of prisoners sitting where we had left them.

'He looks so depressed,' said one about the boy they had visited. She was pregnant.

'Yeah, they all look so lost,' said the other.

'I always look back,' said the first. I had not thought to do so but now I turned. Tuggy Tug was gazing at me. He broke into a grin of relief.

Twenty-two

While Tuggy Tug was in prison, his elderly foster mother Daphne invited me to tea. She was very upset at what had happened to him. She had six children of her own, countless grandchildren and even great-grandchildren as well as the numerous children she had fostered – but she still worried about Tuggy Tug and sent him money in jail.

We sat in her sitting room on a gilt sofa set with gold cushions, photographs of children on every side table, propped along the bookcase and placed among candles on top of the baby grand piano. She offered me home-made biscuits and poured tea from a teapot covered in rosebuds. It was a Sunday in autumn. As on every Sunday, she had spent the morning in church and planned to go again in the evening.

This was the house where Tuggy Tug had spent six years of his childhood. It was where he had returned after lunch with Bobby Cummines to show his nan he was ready to change.

I had gone back now to try and understand.

Daphne sipped her tea and picked over why the engaging child she had loved had ended up a criminal.

She talked of Tuggy Tug's mother and her five children. Daphne was firm: 'Why did the authorities not stop her having children? How can they allow this to continue when they know what those children suffered from their birth? Presumably she loved them but she can't bring herself to leave the drugs, poor soul.'

She moved on to social services. Twenty years of fostering and 'I seen the whole cycle. Social workers want to work one-on-one with a child. Instead they are like a ball rolling around between too many children and they are so inexperienced, God help them. You have to do so much of their work for them.'

She recalled Tuggy Tug arriving aged five as an emergency placement in the middle of the night with his sister. He had already been with one foster carer and was 'by now very disturbed. He and his sister just kept on crying and crying. It went on for days like that.'

Lack of experience and training meant social workers tend to cling to orthodoxies, said Daphne, stirring her tea. They lack the confidence to exercise judgement and common sense. They believe, for example, that siblings should remain together. So when the sister's new foster mother wanted to adopt the girl – 'the woman took her on holidays abroad and treated her like a daughter' – social services refused. Daphne said, 'They should listen to foster parents. They know what is good for the child.'

When it came to keeping the birth mother in contact with her children, however, nothing was too much trouble for social services. Daphne was puzzled. One moment the child is in so much peril they remove it from its mother, 'The next social services are arranging visits.' The mother would turn up, 'bringing so many different presents, among them odd shoes, pieces of fruit – all stolen. She would excite him with these big promises to return in a month but she never did. Twice social services allowed her to build up the child – only to let him down. Tugs never took it lightly.'

She went out to make a fresh pot. As the fourth of five children, all of whom had been taken into care, 'Why was he not removed straight away and adopted?' mused Daphne on her return. We both knew why. Social services believe only black couples should adopt black children, but black couples are in short supply. We allowed ourselves to daydream. What if Tuggy Tug had been adopted as a baby by a couple – whatever their race or colour? He would have had the chance of a loving and secure upbringing, a decent education and would, by now, be on his way to achieving that dream of a good job and a house in the suburbs.

Social services believe this would have caused racial confusion. It might well have done. Given the choice, he might have decided that racial confusion was a preferable alternative to a prison cell at eighteen.

We sighed and reminisced about Tuggy Tug. She recalled his unexpected arrival in the suit and his pride. She said, 'I prayed to God someone would take him on.' I said I had failed him. She urged me not to give up, to keep visiting him. 'Let him feel good; tell him how good he can be. I fostered so many children. So many of them start good like Tugs and I have seen how we turn them bad. He is so kind and loving. He could change. I gave him money but he refused to take it. He's got something there.' She sighed. 'He's so lonely in this world. His gang is some company. Individually they are angels but together they are vicious.'

I stood up to leave and Daphne walked me to the front door. She could not let Tuggy Tug go. She assured me, 'He can't mash an ant he's so soft. Such a softie but he will try and put on a show.' We came out into the fragile light of an October evening. Someone shouted. Briefly Daphne's face lit up – 'I hear his voice!' She listened. 'No? OK,' she said and waved me off.

As I drove back across the river, the rain blurred the neon lights of the London Eye into a halo of blue, and I reflected on what the past three years among the hoods had taught me. By accident I had got to know one gang of boys over a crucial period of their lives. I had watched my son go through the same transition. At the start of his secondary school the headmaster had addressed us. The next five years were of enormous importance in our sons' lives, he had said. Together, school and parents shared an onerous responsibility – turning thirteen-year-olds into men. The headmaster's words struck me forcibly. I had obsessed about potty training and bedtimes. In contrast I had not, until that speech, given my son's teenage years much thought – except as a bout of bad weather to be endured. Fortunately, his school had.

There are always going to be young men who are just bad. I sat opposite one on a train from Newcastle. Between us was a row of mini-bottles of alcohol, which he was going through one by one. He was a twenty-two-year-old Royal Marine who had done two tours of duty in Afghanistan and one in Iraq. He described with relish what it felt like to get a man in his sights. There is no reason for his aggression. He comes from a loving family. His sister is a vet and his brother an accountant. He just enjoyed killing.

That soldier is the exception. He is one of the small minority of young men who are never going to fit easily into society. The tragedy is we are turning a large number of potentially decent young men into misfits and criminals. When I first met Tuggy Tug outside the chicken takeaway, he did not have to be one of them. Neither did Smalls, Sunshine, Bulldog or Lips; and neither in the future do Pocket and Tshane.

Tuggy Tug and his gang were first failed by their parents then by every institution that is supposed to care. As Bulldog said, 'I was fucked over by my mum and dad then fucked over by the state. I don't know which was worse.'

We sneer at the obsession with celebrity culture, winning the lottery, getting on *Big Brother* or becoming a rap star. But boys like Tuggy Tug are not stupid. They know, even if we do not, that getting on *Big Brother* is more likely than changing their lives for the better. We have left them no path upwards.

A TV presenter once asked me at a party if it was not wrong to force middle-class values on boys like Tuggy Tug. But what is Tuggy Tug's dream – a house in the suburbs, membership to a golf club – if not of middle-class success? How is he to achieve this, despite his qualities, without self-discipline and application? These attributes need not be dictated by intelligence, class or privilege. They may be a lot easier to acquire if your parents have them. But they can be learnt anywhere and by anyone. They do not require government spending, an extra tier of professionals or spanking-new facilities. What they do require is an education establishment convinced of their importance. Failure of schools to teach them is condemning teenage boys from poor backgrounds to a lifetime of wasted opportunities.

We wonder why the rioters we saw in the summer of 2011 reject our society. But what experience have rioters like Mash, Bulldog and Sunshine had of our state institutions – not to mention charities – but incompetence and indifference? When I told the boys I was shocked by what I had learnt from going with them to the job centre, for example, they were incredulous. Smalls said, 'But everyone knows what them places are like.' The trouble is most of us do not. We spend £100 billion a year on welfare but are unable to feed, house or educate large numbers of adolescents on our inner-city streets – until, that is, they go to prison.

We cannot continue to warehouse generation after generation of young men without a repetition of the violence of the summer of 2011.

Shortly after my tea with Daphne, I heard Smalls had been arrested. He was sentenced to four years for drug dealing.

Meanwhile I managed to get Mash an interview for a job in

a gym. We met in Acre Lane on a cool autumn afternoon. He took my breath away. In the months I had not seen him, Mash had transformed from a boy into a man – and a very well-dressed man. He was wearing heavy patent leather shoes with jeans and a cashmere top by a French designer. It was black with four tiny pearl buttons at the throat and a band of jostled images across the stomach. My broker friends wore clothes by the same designer to demonstrate both their wealth and street cred. Mash sat legs akimbo giving me his slow smile throughout the interview. Afterwards we joked together, but on the first day of work he never turned up. He never answered my phone calls. I was devastated.

Swagger was less surprised. 'He just wants to be like his uncle and his dad. They're known faces in the hood. From that top, looks like he's on his way. He's unreachable now.' I said I always felt I had more influence on Mash than on Tuggy Tug. He listened to me. Swagger snorted. 'I don't see no listening. I just see him pulling the wool over your eyes. And he thinks he's good at it. I told you one would end up in prison and one would end up in a designer suit. Mash was always smart, manipulated you, got off court, not got a criminal record and now is goin' around in designer gear!'

I had never seen Swagger so bitter and depressed. Tuggy Tug's incarceration had hit him hard. At the same time, he had not seen his child for months. He had no one to look after any more. 'I am under a lot of pressure,' he admitted. He was smoking more weed. He had lost weight and now weighed less than ten stone. His designer clothes hung off him and stubble disfigured his once-gleaming head. He planned to go to Jamaica for Christmas. He called me later. He had finally got to talk to Tshane. 'Daddy no go, no go,' the child had said.

'Well don't,' I said. I was losing patience with this new Swagger. He sighed. 'My ticker's giving me trouble. I need a break, man.'

He rang me a few days later. He had paid off the last instalment of his ticket. He had called his girlfriend and asked to speak to Tshane but she had refused and told him not to call again. She added that she planned to leave London after Christmas for good. 'I am in bits,' said Swagger. 'Where will she take him? How will I find him?' Suddenly I heard sobbing. 'What is to become of Tshane, Harry? What is to become of me?'

I was wrong about Tuggy Tug too. In the new year, I asked Mark for the rushes of the BBC documentary that had never been made. By then I was trying to make sense of all that had happened. I sat down to watch the DVD on my own one night. Outside it was bitterly cold, with a full moon blurred by wind-driven cloud.

I did not expect Tuggy Tug to say much about me. After all, what had I done for him? I had shown him another world, persuaded him of its worth then failed to help him reach it. But in this, as in so many things, he surprised me.

Mark had interviewed Tuggy Tug on his estate. In the gloom of a stairwell, Tuggy Tug turns towards the camera. He is in a new brown hoodie, far too big for him and gorgeously decorated with a green and gold skull wearing a top hat. One of Tuggy Tug's hands protectively cups some weed while his other lifts and crumbles the drug.

Mark steadies the camera and asks when he first saw me. 'Met her outside the chicken shop,' recalled Tuggy Tug. 'It was nice that day. Must have been years ago. We were just jamming outside chicken shop one day. Bare man . . . broke fam. I was hungry everything fam. She helped me out . . .'

When I offered to take them to eat, 'I'm thinking only three of us can come cos there's not enough space in her car innit. But

I could have brought every man that's how kind she was, get me. Shouted three of us. You know and I'm picking wisely. I wanna fiver, I just want a fiver out of their money,' for including them. 'And you know from there I thought I'll never see this woman again in my life. Forget me, she'll never phone me cos she's got bare money. Why would she phone me?'

But I had. 'You know what it feels like when you see her number coming up? If you had a baller [a rich person] that phoned your phone up, you answer. Why would you miss that call bruv?

'At first I thought she was like a money opportunist yeah, I could just get money and that. But you see now she proper help me like getting me jobs and that's worth more than any money she could give me.

'She always helps me, she always phones me, there's always something for me to do. She could have just phoned me, I could have helped her with one thing, she would never have known me. She really wanted to know me. You get me? So she is a good friend and that.'

Mark emphasises that I am from a different world, 'She's quite posh isn't she?' Tuggy Tug puts him right. 'Posh don't mean nothing. It's good to know someone who is like that. See if you know people like that yeah in your heart it makes you feel like you're meant to get there innit?' Lips dawdles into view and Tuggy Tug pulls him over for confirmation. 'Feel me, if you knew someone who's posh that was sitting on cake and she phoned you and helped you . . . you hear me? I can never disrespect her for that. This woman,' he says with complete conviction – affection and finance balled up into one – 'will never leave me broke.'

At the time when we met, 'I was on a tenner, twenty pound, five pound, that's how young I was,' recalled Tuggy Tug, who even reckoned his age in the amounts he was making. 'So obviously when I heard money I was just happy innit, thinking this was just gonna be a one-time. I never expected it to go this far. So now that it's gone this far I don't really care about money no more, when it comes to her. We're past that. She helps my friends, certain ones of my friends, been cool with us. So she does help me.' He paused and then this young man to whom wealth is everything says, 'There are things that are worth more than money. You get me?'

The rushes end with the walk we took along the Thames at Richmond two springs before. Apart from the encounter with the lady and her poodle, we also met Audley Harrison, the first British boxer to win an Olympic gold in the super heavyweight division. Originally from Brixton, he paused to talk to us. 'Raise your game. You got to raise your game,' he tells an infatuated Tuggy Tug, his eyes huge as he licks his ice cream.

We walk on and come across a painter, a small Italian at an easel by the side of the river, painting the path and the cherry trees. Tuggy Tug stares for a moment. 'Hey I just clocked what he's painting you know, look at that!' he exclaims. 'Oh it looks sick! Hey you're sick!' The little painter thanks him politely. 'He's painting the cherry blossom,' says Swagger.

'They only last one week,' says the painter.

'One week!' says Swagger.

'Even,' says the painter.

Tuggy Tug asks if he has been painting long. The artist replies thirty-two years. 'How long?' asks Tuggy Tug, taken aback.

'Thirty-two years,' repeats the artist.

'Thirty-two years,' says Tuggy Tug.

'Yes,' says the artist.

'It didn't happen overnight?' asks Tuggy Tug.

'No, no, no,' says the artist.

I buy the painting and Swagger asks him to put us in. He sits us on a low wall except for Tuggy Tug. He insists on standing next to the easel so he can watch the painter at work. 'Can you put me in there as well boss? But I don't want to sit over there. Can't you just put it in for me?' He stares riveted, calling over progress to us as the painter explains what he is doing. 'He's making an outline,' reports Tuggy Tug. The painter describes how to mix colours. 'A touch of white and you can see the hoodie there!' Tuggy Tug exclaims. 'What's this part with the sleeves?' He hurries over to join us then rushes back to inspect the result. 'Sick, blud!' he says to the painter in wonder. 'You put some real skills in this blud, are you nuts?'

Swagger walks over to join them. He smiles, shakes his head and says, 'Any time I want to come to Richmond and I don't have the money, now I can look at this painting and remember this day.'

So there we are sitting on a low wall, a perfect spring day, a splurge of pink cherry blossom above us.

It is I, as it turns out, who am the only one of us to look at that painting; and I look at it often.

Swagger's prophecy proved correct. Mash ended up in designer clothes. Bulldog was sectioned. Tuggy Tug, Lips, Smalls and Jiggers are all in prison – Jiggers for shooting and wounding a young man. On his first night in prison, as I later learnt, Tuggy Tug tried to kill himself. It took three guards to save him.

For Swagger that holiday in Jamaica proved fatal. He was misdiagnosed and died there from septicaemia. He died alone. As Tuggy Tug remarked, sitting in the sunshine on that wall, 'Your life's due to end one day. End. It's just when fam.'

'Yeah,' replies Swagger, 'but it's how. How.' The moment catches the heart then dissolves and moves on. Tuggy Tug made us laugh and the black poodle bounced into view.

Postscript

This book is a description of my three-year friendship with one gang. It is taken from my diary and notes and from research for two reports I wrote for the Centre For Policy Studies, 'Handle with Care: An Investigation into the Care System' (2006) and 'Wasted: The Betrayal of White Working-Class and Black Caribbean Boys'. (2009) My friendship with Swagger and then later with Tuggy Tug and his gang provided me with the anger to write those reports. I included many of their observations. This book is a truthful account, with a few exceptions. The visit to the Imperial War Museum draws on two separate trips. Swagger's and my experience of charities came at an earlier date while researching 'Handle with Care'. Tuggy Tug's gang had a white member called Bulldog but the character of Bulldog himself is based on another white member of a black gang who I befriended while researching 'Handle with Care'. A few details are changed in order to protect certain individuals and some characters have been merged for brevity. I never taped Tuggy Tug (except for lunch at the Liberal Club when by chance I was experimenting with the apps on my new iPhone). I am therefore deeply grateful to the BBC and the independent TV production company CTVC for allowing me to use the rushes from their tasters. I hope they show why his company was always a delight.

Acknowledgements

I am deeply grateful to the following people: Tessa Keswick for commissioning me to write for the Centre For Policy Studies; Tim Knox, the present director; Paul Dacre who asked me to investigate black Caribbean and white working-class boys; Susannah Herbert who first got me to write about Tuggy Tug and Martin Ivens who has allowed me to continue; and Tim Binding who had the idea for the book.

I am also grateful for guidance and inspiration to Clovis and Jacky Reid, Marlon Campbell and my daughter Gabriella who is always my first reader. This book is for the lost boys who told me their stories. And to the memory of Keith Reid, 1970–2011.